THE BEST
MINNESOTA
SPORTS
ARGUMENTS

THE 100 MOST CONTROVERSIAL, DEBATABLE QUESTIONS FOR DIE-HARD FANS

BOB SANSEVERE

SOURCEBOOKS, INC.
NAPERVILLE, ILLINOIS

Published by Sourcebooks, Inc.

P.O. Box 4410, Naperville, Illinois 60567-4410

(630) 961-3900

Fax: (630) 961-2168

www.sourcebooks.com

Library of Congress Cataloging-in-Publication Data
Sansevere, Bob.
  The best Minnesota sports arguments : the 100 most controversial, debatable questions for die-hard fans / Bob Sansevere.
    p. cm.
  ISBN 978-1-4022-1061-7 (pbk.)
  1. Sports—Minnesota—History. I. Title.
GV584.M65S26 2007
796.09776—dc22

                                                                2007026022

Printed and bound in the United States of America.

CH 10 9 8 7 6 5 4 3 2 1

For Mary and the kids
(Samantha, Sawyer, Spencer, and Shane)

CONTENTS

THE BEST MINNESOTA SPORTS ARGUMENTS

THE BEST MINNESOTA SPORTS ARGUMENTS

INTRODUCTION

Arguments can ensue at any time. They could be in a barroom, a backroom, a bedroom, a bathroom, or any room anywhere. This book takes sides in 100 of the biggest and best arguments related to sports in Minnesota. You may agree, which means you are extremely bright and know a sound, solid argument when you hear one. Or, you may disagree, which does not mean you're a lamebrain. It just means you don't know a sound, solid argument when you hear one.

Who's on first? That's not an argument in this book. It's a famous Abbott & Costello comedy routine.

Who's first? Now, that comes up a lot in the book. For instance: Who was Minnesota's best homegrown hockey player? We're not telling you here. But keep reading.

Get past these first couple of pages and you'll find reasons to agree, and disagree.

There are arguments related to the Vikings.

And the Twins.

And the Timberwolves.

And the Wild.

The Gophers, too.

And also arguments about teams no longer with us, such as the North Stars, the Lakers, the Millers, and even the Pike, who took the pipe after just one season.

Several arguments are related to Kirby Puckett. There are arguments about his home runs bringing tears of joy and arguments about his home wrecking bringing tears to Tonya.

Besides arguments involving Puck, there also are arguments about puck.

And luck.

And pluck.

There are arguments about a Walker (Herschel) and a trotter (Dan Patch).

And arguments about the Miracle on Ice and misery on the lake.

And arguments about a coach named Gags and a team that gagged.

There's one argument that includes Eddie Guardado and El Guapo, and another that's about Bronko.

Who's more deserving of being in baseball's Hall of Fame, Bert Blyleven or Jack Morris? We'll tell you.

We'll also tell you which athletes playing today are most likely to be in the Hall of Fame some day.

Who's the most selfish athlete ever to play for a Minnesota team? We'll tell you that, too.

How did we get so smart about Minnesota sports?

Well, it started at a 5,000-watt radio station in Fresno, California. Actually, that's where Ted Baxter, the WJM-TV anchorman on *The Mary Tyler Moore Show*, got his start. For the longest time, much of what I knew about Minnesota I knew from watching Ted, Mary Richards, Lou Grant, and other

MTM cast members.

In other words, I didn't know much.

I was living in New Jersey. Other than during the playoffs, the Vikings rarely were on TV. Back in Jersey in the 1970s and 1980s, you'd get the Giants and the Jets on the tube and not much else. Then, in 1984, I was hired to cover the Vikings for the *Minneapolis Star Tribune*. My first season on the beat, I covered the Les Steckel Error. I covered some interesting teams and intriguing people. You'll read about some of them in the pages that follow. A few years later, I became a sports columnist at the *St. Paul Pioneer Press*. I also began talking about sports on the KQRS Morning Show. I have covered just about everything and everyone involved in sports in Minnesota for the past two decades: two World Series, the Love Boat scandal, the Gophers' cheating scandal, good Vikings teams, bad Vikings teams, Denny, Red, and Norm Green.

I was there for all of it, pen and pad in hand, with my computer revved up and ready.

I have interviewed and written about many of the athletes, coaches, and team owners and officials mentioned in this book. Most of the quotes in the book attributed to the *Pioneer Press* were from interviews I conducted.

But that's enough about me.

It's time for the arguments to begin.

PRO
FOOTBALL

WHY ARE THE VIKINGS MORE POPULAR THAN THE TWINS?

1 George Carlin once did a comedy routine comparing baseball and football. He said, "Baseball begins in the spring, the season of new life. Football begins in the fall, when everything's dying."

That gives you a pretty good idea which sport Carlin preferred.

In cities such as New York and Boston, sports fans are passionate about all of their football and baseball teams. But if New Yorkers had to choose one sport over the other, the Yankees and Mets would win out over the Giants and Jets. In Boston, it's not even a contest—Red Sox over Patriots.

In Minnesota, it's the other way. The Vikings are No. 1. The Twins are entrenched at No. 2. After those two, among professional teams, it's the Wild at No. 3 and the Timberwolves at No. 4. And that's the way it will stay, except for the occasional playoff run when fans squint more closely at whatever team is in the postseason.

For example, the only times the Twins leapfrogged the Vikings in popularity were in 1987 and 1991, when they won the World Series. Minnesota fans didn't care at all about the Vikings in October of 1987. But that mostly had to do with the fact that, while the Twins were in the postseason, the Vikings were fielding a team of misfits and castoffs to play games during a strike by the real players.

The Vikings cemented their hold on No. 1 in the hearts, minds, and wallets of Minnesota fans when Bud Grant became their coach in 1967 and began leading them to division titles and Super Bowls. It's not just a throwaway line: everybody does like a winner, and the Vikings were winners for most of Grant's tenure as coach.

The Vikings also played in an open-air stadium for most of that period. In Carlin's routine, he said, "Football is played in any kind of weather: Rain, snow, sleet, hail, fog. In baseball, if it rains, we don't go out to play." Minnesotans like to go out and play in any kind of weather, and the Vikings' appeal had something to do with the Grant-era teams playing outside in the coldest of weather and Minnesotans being hearty and outdoorsy. Many Minnesotans embrace the wintry chill by going outdoors to ski, skate, ice fish, snowmobile, and play hockey and broomball, and they saw the Vikings as an extension of themselves.

They connected, and the connection remained after the Vikings moved into the Metrodome. It remains to this very day, to this very nanosecond.

WHO WAS THE WORST TEAMMATE IN MINNESOTA SPORTS HISTORY?

2 As if it wasn't enough that he had world-class speed and Inspector Gadget arms that could reach way up and pluck   almost any ball out of the air, Randy Moss knew how to get an added edge. When the Vikings played home games at the Metrodome, Moss would watch himself on the jumbo video screens located behind each end zone. As he ran downfield, he looked at the video screen for when the ball was in the air. And then he caught it.

And often, he scored with it.

In nationally televised games, Moss's adrenal glands would put in overtime and, usually, he would put up magnificent numbers.

He particularly liked Thanksgiving Day games in Dallas. Peeved that the Cowboys didn't pick him in the draft, Moss scalded Dallas his rookie year with 3 touchdown catches of more than 50 yards each. Two years later, he scorched the Cowboys yet again. This time, he had 7 receptions for 144 yards and 2 touchdowns. On a 52-yard bomb, he beat triple coverage.

When Moss wanted to play, nobody was better. Not now. Not ever.

The thing is, Moss didn't always want to play.

His infamous line haunts him to this day: "I play when I want to play."

There were days he loafed on the field, days he didn't block or care if he made a catch. One time, against the Redskins, he walked off the field before the game was over. That chapped the hides of fellow Vikings. Teammates will put up with a lot, particularly from a talented player. But quitting, that's a tough one for them to swallow.

Moss didn't exactly endear himself to teammates when he showboated, either. There was that time in Green Bay when he scored and then made believe he was pulling down his pants to moon fans at Lambeau Field. Many teammates just wanted him to keep his pants up and his mind on catching passes and winning games.

There have been other Minnesota athletes who weren't particularly liked by teammates. A number of players from the Vikings' Purple People Eaters days weren't fond of Fran Tarkenton. He was distant, and too aloof. And Christian Laettner, when he was with the Timberwolves, didn't host a lot of tea parties for teammates. He was a snippy one, that Laettner.

But guys like Tarkenton and Laettner at least put in an honest effort when they were in games. You can't say that about ol' Randy. He had a knack for tormenting opponents and teammates alike. He also showed little regard for his coaches. You don't really coach a guy like Randy Moss. What you do is hope he doesn't create too much discord in the locker room.

And when he does, when he becomes a monstrous pain in the kiester, you do what Mike Tice did after the 2004 season. You trade him for whatever you can get. The Vikings got the seventh overall pick in the 2005 draft as well as linebacker Napoleon Harris.

To some, it didn't seem like nearly enough for a player with Moss's talent. To others, including some teammates, it was more than enough just to get rid of the guy.

WHAT WAS THE MOST DISAPPOINTING LOSS IN MINNESOTA SPORTS HISTORY?

3 Ask any Vikings fan if they remember the 1998 NFC Championship Game and they'll groan. Or they'll shake their heads, shake their fists, or say, "Why the #%&*@$ did they take a knee?" Or, they will do all of those things.

That championship game between the Vikings and Atlanta Falcons remains a raw nerve for many Minnesotans.

During the regular season in 1998, the Vikings went 15–1

and set the NFL scoring record with 556 points. They didn't score fewer than 24 points in any game, and that included their only loss that season to Tampa Bay. The Vikings stomped teams behind a rejuvenated Randall Cunningham and a rookie wide receiver named Randy Moss, who led the league with 17 touchdown catches.

In the NFC title game, the Vikings were favored by double digits. Beating the Falcons was supposed to be little more than a formality. No 15–1 team had ever failed to make it to the Super Bowl. And the Vikings were playing at the Metrodome, one of the loudest stadiums in the league and one of the toughest for opposing teams because of that noise. The Vikings were supposed to go to the Super Bowl for the fifth time in franchise history and win it this time. They were supposed to be a team of destiny. Unfortunately, it turned out their destiny was to botch things up.

Things were looking good for the Vikings early in the fourth quarter of that championship game. They led by 10 points. Even after the Falcons whittled the lead to seven with a field goal, the Vikings and their fans weren't in panic mode. Cunningham drove them 55 yards for what looked to be an easy 38-yard field goal with 2:07 left. Gary Anderson hadn't missed a field goal attempt all season. He had kicked 16 of his 39 field goals that season from farther than 38 yards, including a 53- and 50-yarder. A 38-yarder was practically a gimme for him.

He missed it. The ball was wide left by less than a foot.

Suddenly, it got quieter than a mortuary inside the

7

Metrodome. Instead of a 10-point lead and a lock on that fifth journey to the Super Bowl, the Vikings were vulnerable. And the Falcons were energized. They drove 71 yards and tied the score on a Chris Chandler-to-Terance Mathis touchdown pass.

But there still were 49 seconds to play in the 4th quarter. That was plenty of time for one of the most explosive offenses in NFL history. The Vikings still could win the game if they drove into range for a field goal.

There was one problem with that. Vikings coach Denny Green made one of the all-time boneheaded decisions a coach has ever made in any sport. Facing a 3rd-and-3 from his own 27, and with 30 seconds left in the game, he had Cunningham take a knee.

Green had this great high-scoring and powerful offense and he chose to drain the clock and play for overtime.

If anyone ever calls a decision of yours idiotic, just tell them at least it's not as idiotic as Denny Green's decision to have Cunningham take a knee.

The Falcons won 30–27 in overtime on Morten Andersen's 38-yard field goal. Note the yardage; it was the same distance from which Gary Anderson failed.

It's not the fact that the Vikings didn't win the Super Bowl that year. Heck, the Vikings have lost four Super Bowls and the Twins lost in the 1965 World Series. Those were disappointing losses, but at least those Vikings and Twins teams had a chance to play for the title.

The 1998 Vikings blew that chance, which is why that loss

in the conference championship game wasn't just disappointing. It was the most disappointing loss in the long and storied history of Minnesota sports.

WHICH OUT-OF-TOWN ATHLETE STUCK THE BIGGEST DAGGER IN THE HEARTS OF MINNESOTANS?

4 Sandy Koufax put a hurting on the Twins and their fans in the 1965 World Series. The Los Angeles Dodgers ace beat the Twins not once, but twice. Ouch.

Koufax allowed just 4 singles and struck out 10 in a 7–0 rout in Game 5. Then, on two days' rest, he struck out 10 again—and struck down the hopes of the Twins and their followers. This was Game 7, and Koufax threw a 3-hit shutout in a 2–0 win.

It left an ache.

But it was nothing compared to the damage done to the Minnesota psyche a decade later by a Dallas Cowboys wide receiver named Drew "Effing" Pearson. In much the same way New York Yankees shortstop Bucky Dent is called Bucky "Effing" Dent by Boston Red Sox fans for the way he crunched their World Series hopes with a wind-aided home run in the 1978 American League East division playoff game, Pearson is reviled by Vikings fans who were around in 1975.

Minnesotans love the Twins whenever the Twins are winning and there's a chance for another World Series championship. Otherwise, they just like the Twins.

But Minnesotans always are passionate about the Vikings, through good times and bad. That's why what Pearson did still gnaws at the innards of Vikings fans old enough to recall it. Actually, any Vikings fan worth his weight in Fran Tarkenton bobbleheads knows all about Drew "Effing" Pearson, whether or not he or she had yet to be born in 1975.

With just 36 seconds left in the NFC divisional playoff game on the Vikings' home tundra at Metropolitan Stadium, Pearson caught a 50-yard touchdown pass from Roger Staubach that is remembered as the Hail Mary pass by some and "That Lousy, Stinking, Cheating Reception" by others.

Cowboys fans will tell you what Pearson did was fair and square. Vikings fans will howl that he pushed off cornerback Nate Wright and should have been penalized for offensive pass interference.

What everyone will agree on is that, with the Vikings ahead 14–10, Wright was in single coverage against Pearson down the right sideline, and that there was contact between Pearson and Wright. Wright fell, Pearson caught the ball on his right hip, and he traipsed into the end zone.

Dallas won 17–14.

One of the few people in the stadium as unpopular as Pearson was the game referee, Armen Terzian. He got conked on the head by a whiskey bottle hurled out of the stands. While he was soaked in blood, the Vikings and their fans were soaked in anger that neither Terzian nor any other official threw a flag against Pearson.

The Cowboys went on to play in Super Bowl X, where they lost to the Pittsburgh Steelers. Had the Vikings beaten the Cowboys, they could have made their third straight Super Bowl appearance and, this time, they had a team good enough to win. The 1975 Vikings went 12–2 during the regular season and, as then-coach Bud Grant recalled in the *St. Paul Pioneer Press*, "The 1975 team that didn't go to the Super Bowl might have been as dominant a team as we ever had. The thing you remember is Drew Pearson caught the (game-winning touchdown) pass. Now, had Pearson not caught that pass, the thing you'd be writing about is the great drive we put on to go ahead. I think with six minutes to go we were on our 20-yard line. We marched down the field, converting 3rd downs and using the clock. It was as good a drive as we'd ever put on. We score (with 1:51 left). That would have been the signature of the game. Nobody remembers. I remember it. That's what you would be writing about, rather than the Pearson play. We might have won the Super Bowl."

On behalf of Vikings fans everywhere: Damn that Drew "Effing" Pearson.

11

OF ALL THE VIKINGS' GREAT DEFENSIVE LINEMEN, WHO WOULD MAKE UP THEIR ALL-TIME GREATEST FRONT FOUR?

5 Alan Page and Carl Eller are in the Pro Football Hall of Fame. Those two Purple People Eaters are slam-dunk members of the Vikings' all-time greatest front four. Though they played in the 1960s and 1970s, both would be exceptional in today's game. We're talking all-pro caliber.

Page was a tackle, Eller an end. It was tough to run inside because of Page, and Eller turned more than a few quarterbacks into human mulch after blowing past an offensive tackle. Eller holds the Vikings' record for most sacks in a career with 130, and Page was no slouch when it came to tormenting quarterbacks. He had 18 sacks in 1976, an incredible number for a tackle, and he led the Vikings in sacks in six separate seasons.

Page and Eller were good, damn good.

Based on longevity, fellow Purple People Eater Jim Marshall should join Page and Eller on that all-time greatest front four. However, he doesn't make the cut.

Marshall played defensive end opposite Eller on those Vikings teams that went to four Super Bowls. 'Ol Jim was good, real good, but he loses out to Chris Doleman on this front four of ours.

When he first joined the Vikings as a first-round draft choice out of Pittsburgh in 1985, Doleman was miscast as an outside linebacker. Once he moved to end, he became one of the league's most feared pass rushers. In 1989, Doleman led the league with 21 sacks, which remains the Vikings' franchise record for quarterback smack downs.

One huge reason Doleman was so successful was because Keith Millard lined up beside him at tackle. Eller had Page, and Doleman had Millard. Different eras, same result: a lot of sacks.

In the season Doleman had 21 sacks, Millard had 18. There was no better tackle-end tandem on any defense than Eller and Page in the late 1960s and 1970s. And in the 1980s, there were none better than Doleman and Millard.

John Randle came along in the 1990s, and he was a very good defensive lineman who racked up quite a few sacks. He just wasn't as good as Eller, Doleman, Page, or Millard. In other words, he just wasn't good enough to crack this all-time greatest Vikings front four we've assembled.

The Los Angeles Rams once had a front four called The Fearsome Foursome. If Eller, Page, Doleman, and Millard could have played together, it wouldn't just have been fearsome. It also would have been a formidable foursome.

WERE THE VIKINGS RESPONSIBLE FOR THE DALLAS COWBOYS' MINI-DYNASTY IN THE 1990s?

6 So were they? Were the Vikings really responsible for the Dallas Cowboys winning three Super Bowls in four years?

Well, as they say down Texas way, yup.

Jerry Jones and Jimmy Johnson take credit for assembling those Super Bowl teams, but the true architect of those three Cowboy championships was Vikings general manager Mike Lynn.

When Lynn made the dopiest trade of all time, the Herschel Walker trade, he gave the Cowboys the ammo they needed to become world champions.

Mike Lynn was not a stupid man, except for that one day in October 1989 when he acquired Walker from the Cowboys. You ever hear of a TV or an appliance going on the fritz? Something like that must have happened to Lynn's brain, because it sure stopped functioning properly.

It wasn't enough that Lynn shipped five players to Dallas for Walker. Stupidly, he also sent along a slew of draft choices, including a first-round choice in 1992. There also were conditional first-round picks in 1990 and 1991, conditional second-round picks in 1990, 1991, and 1992, and a conditional third-round selection in 1992.

Lynn had all those conditional picks tied to the players he swapped to the Cowboys for Walker, who wasn't much more than an above-average running back. The way the deal was structured, the Cowboys could keep either the players or the draft picks. Lynn screwed up by figuring Jones and Johnson would want the players, who included running back Darrin Nelson, linebackers Jesse Solomon and David Howard, and cornerback Issiac Holt.

Lynn figured wrong.

Jones and Johnson didn't want the Vikings' castoffs. They wanted the picks, not the players, and used those draft picks to assemble their Super Bowl teams. The Cowboys packaged the Vikings' picks as well as their own and others they acquired to teams that traded them even more draft picks.

Bottom line: All those Vikings' draft choices enabled the Cowboys to wheel and deal and acquire the likes of running back Emmitt Smith, defensive tackle Russell Maryland, cornerback Kevin Smith, and safety Darren Woodson. All were vital members of the Cowboys' Super Bowl-winning teams after the 1992, 1993, and 1995 seasons.

And it was all because of Mike Lynn.

WHO WAS MINNESOTA'S WORST COACH/MANAGER?

7 You want the truth? You want the whole truth? You want nothing but the truth?

OK, here it is. The competition isn't even close when it comes to the worst coach or manager in the history of Minnesota sports.

There were some inept coaches of Minnesota teams. Jimmy Rodgers, Sidney Lowe, and Bill Blair all lasted less than two full seasons as Timberwolves coaches and not one of them had a winning percentage above .265. In fact, Rodgers' winning percentage was a pathetic .189. Ray Miller was such a lousy Twins manager he was fired with only a handful of games left in the 1986 season. And then there was Norm Van Brocklin, the Vikings' first coach. He was a Hall of Fame quarterback but nothing special as a coach. In six seasons under Van Brocklin, the Vikings went 29–51–4.

The worst of them all, though, was Les Steckel.

He coached the Vikings for just one season . . . one putrid season.

It's not remembered as the Steckel Era. It was the Steckel Error.

The Vikings went 3–13 in 1984, Steckel's lone season. If you think George Orwell's *1984* was scary, you should have been around for Steckel's.

He was going to change the way NFL coaches did things. He had all the answers. Anyway, that's what he thought.

A Marine officer who served in Vietnam before becoming a coach, Steckel tried transferring to the football field what he learned in the military. On the Vikings' first day of training camp under Steckel, the players didn't run plays. They ran an obstacle course.

He couldn't be more different than the legend he replaced, Bud Grant. Bud was an Xs and Os guy, a Paul Brown disciple. Meanwhile, Steckel believed in disciples, ones with names like Matthew, Mark, and Luke. Besides having that Marine mentality, Steckel also wanted to assemble a team loaded with Christians. That's right. He wanted to coach the God Squad. Some players didn't know if it was more important to carry a playbook or a Bible. Others refused to buy into what Steckel was preaching.

Steckel's theatrics weren't just Biblical: Early on, he cut a credit card in half. It was his way of telling players he was putting an end to what he perceived as a country-club atmosphere. To make another point, he punched himself in the face.

This was not the coach the Vikings and their fans expected, or wanted, to see. Not yet 40, Steckel had been the Vikings' wide receivers coach under Grant. He was a surprise choice because of his age and because he hadn't been a coordinator. He wasn't handpicked by Grant, if you're wondering. Grant tilted toward his long-time offensive coordinator, Jerry Burns. Steckel was General Manager Mike Lynn's selection. (When it comes to blunders in professional sports, Lynn had the market

17

cornered in Minnesota. As mentioned previously, he also orchestrated the Herschel Walker trade some five years later.)

Anyway, after the military-style training camp, the regular season didn't start out so bad. The Vikings opened with losses to San Diego and Philadelphia, then beat Atlanta and Detroit. Then came five losses in a row.

The Vikings beat Tampa Bay 27–24 on November 4. After that win, the team quit on Steckel. They'd grown weary of his tactics and theatrics. Over the final six games, the Vikings were outscored 241–79—an average score of 40–13. If you add in the other ten games, they allowed a franchise-record 484 points and 59 touchdowns. Lynn fired Steckel the day after the season ended. With the incentive of a lifetime contract, Grant was coaxed into coaching the Vikings in 1985. Then, in 1986, Burns got the job that should have been his in 1984.

Years later, after he had become president of the Fellowship of Christian Athletes, Steckel was asked what he would do differently if he could turn the clock back to 1984. He gave an interesting response to the *St. Paul Pioneer Press*: "I wouldn't have accepted the job. As I look back on it, there are some people who are rather mature at age 37. I'm not sure I was. I didn't realize the scope and dimension of being a head coach. I was very sensitive to the fact that some great people, such as Jerry Burns and others, were not offered the job. I was sensitive to it, but not very realistic about it. I made mistakes along the way. Not a few, many."

Apparently, even he knew he was Minnesota's worst coach.

WHAT WAS THE MOST SELFISH ACT COMMITTED BY A MINNESOTA ATHLETE?

8 Let's get right to it. Cris Carter isn't a crook, not in a legal sense, but he did steal from Bill Brown.

In 2003, Carter hijacked from Brown the opportunity to be inducted into the Vikings' Ring of Honor, which pays homage to the franchise's best coaches, players, and personnel in a ceremony held once a year at the Metrodome.

Ordinarily, this wouldn't be such a big deal. However, the way it happened, when it happened, and why it happened makes it the most selfish act by an athlete in Minnesota sports history.

Here's the back story: Brown was supposed to be inducted into the Ring of Honor in 2003. Everything was set. Brown would have his day in front of his wife, Kay, and his four children, as well as his grandchildren, his old teammates, his friends, and about 70,000 fans at the Metrodome.

However, Carter got in touch with Vikings owner Red McCombs. Carter told McCombs he wanted to be inducted into the Ring of Honor in 2003. In fact, Carter insisted on it because, well, he didn't want to wait.

McCombs went along with it and bumped Brown. Carter

played for McCombs and knew him well. Brown came from another era, ending his career long before McCombs owned the franchise. Sure, the Vikings could have avoided this problem by inducting both Carter and Brown in the same season, but they've limited the Ring of Honor to one inductee a year.

What Carter did was wrong, as was what McCombs agreed to do. It was a blow to Bill Brown, causing more pain than any tackler ever had. He didn't want the honor for himself. He wanted it for Kay, who had been married to him for 44 years. She'd been sick for a few years with diabetes. She'd already lost a leg and Bill wanted so much for her to be there with him on what was supposed to be his special day in 2003.

But that day would belong to Carter.

Did Brown raise a stink? Nope. That never was his style. When he played running back in the NFL from 1962 to 1974, he was known as Boom Boom. He didn't elude defenders with fancy moves. He just lowered his crew-cut head and churned those bow legs of his right into defenses. When he lost his starting job, he didn't gripe. He did what he was told and played on special teams.

Bud Grant, his coach back in the day, told the *St. Paul Pioneer Press* that Brown was "very, very gracious" for the way he dealt with Carter leapfrogging him into the Ring of Honor.

Brown did get in a year later, in 2004.

It was different, though.

Kay was gone. She had died that June, on Bill's 66th birthday. It would have been nice, and only right, if Kay could have seen her husband cheered one last time by tens of thousands of Vikings fans.

It would have happened, too, if Cris Carter hadn't hijacked Bill Brown's day.

WAS IT A MISTAKE FOR THE VIKINGS TO MOVE INTO THE METRODOME?

9 Imagine the Green Bay Packers leaving Lambeau Field to play in a domed stadium. It's tough to picture, isn't it?

Well, it used to be just as difficult to envision the Vikings playing indoors.

The Vikings of the 1960s and 1970s were a dominant bunch, and a lot of it had to do with playing outdoors at Metropolitan Stadium after winter set in.

There were no climate-controlled indoor practice facilities then. The Vikings practiced and played in the cold. It gave them a huge advantage.

Ask any player with the Vikings back then about what it was like to play a team from a warm-weather city in December and a smile will crease his face. Those players talk about a team like the Los Angeles Rams, and how those Rams wanted no part of the cold. L.A. players who weren't on the field would be huddled around sideline heaters.

Bud Grant didn't allow sideline heaters. He wanted his players' minds on the game, not on how close they could stand to the heat. He believed his players could stay warm and keep their blood circulating by moving their feet and clapping their hands. And many of the Vikings' linemen played in short sleeves when the thermometer headed south. They weren't crazy. They were playing a mind game, attempting to psych out opponents who were freezing their asses off.

In 21 seasons at the old Metropolitan Stadium, the Vikings had a 97–59–4 record, and that includes all those miserable Norm Van Brocklin teams from the early 1960s. The pre-Metrodome Vikings were 28–8 when the temperature was 32 degrees or colder. In December and January playoff games, the Vikings were 7–3 at the Met—3–0 against the Rams.

If the Vikings could have played their Super Bowls outdoors in cold-weather cities, they actually might have won one.

By the early 1980s, the Vikings needed a new home. Metropolitan Stadium held only 48,446 fans and was better suited for baseball. What the Vikings didn't need was a toasty place where fans could take off their winter coats and opponents had no need for sideline heaters.

When the Vikings moved into the Metrodome in 1982, they didn't just change fields. They leveled the playing field some by surrendering their advantage in cold-weather games. It was smart to move to a new stadium, but it was dumb to move indoors.

WHO WAS THE VIKINGS' BEST AND WORST QUARTERBACK?

10

Believe it or not, it's the same player. There were times when you'd watch Daunte Culpepper having a lousy day playing quarterback for the Vikings and—come on, admit it—you were reminded of Marlon Brando sitting in the backseat of that car in *On the Waterfront* and telling his brother, "You don't understand! I coulda had class. I coulda been a contender. I could've been somebody, instead of a bum, which is what I am."

Culpepper had plenty of days like that, when he played like a bum.

He had plenty of the other days, too, when he played with class and was a contender for the NFL's best quarterback.

Culpepper is what smart people like to call an enigma. He could be great, and he could also be a great disappointment.

In 2004, Culpepper had the best season ever by a Vikings quarterback. He passed for 4,717 yards and 39 touchdowns, and had just 11 interceptions. He was in his fifth season as a full-time starter, and it appeared the only quarterback better than him in the entire league was Peyton Manning of the Indianapolis Colts. And Manning didn't have Culpepper's mobility. Culpepper was 6-foot-4 and, at 265 pounds, bigger than a linebacker. He looked like the prototype for what a quarterback was morphing into in the twenty-first century.

And then came 2005. Before shredding just about every ligament in his knee in the season's seventh game, Culpepper was having a brutal season. He had twice as many interceptions as touchdowns (6 touchdowns and 12 INTs, if you're scoring). He also fumbled the ball a slew of times. There were plays when you would have sworn somebody must have yelled, "Hey, Daunte, that ball's radioactive. You better drop it."

Culpepper wasn't partially responsible for the Vikings' 2–5 start. He was the direct cause of it.

But Vikings coach Mike Tice always had Culpepper's back. He stuck up for him even in the worst of times. However, after the Vikings rallied with a 7–2 record with Culpepper laid up for the rest of the 2005 season, Tice was fired. Culpepper's days with the Vikings were also dwindling. He didn't get along with the new coach, Brad Childress, so he was shipped to Miami in the offseason.

Culpepper came back from the injury faster than even medical people thought possible and began the 2006 season as the Dolphins' starting quarterback. The Dolphins didn't get to see the best of Culpepper, as Vikings fans did in 2004. They got the flip side. They got the worst of Daunte Culpepper; before long, he was benched.

And people wondered, would he ever be a contenda again? Or just a bum?

WHO IS MINNESOTA'S GEORGE BAILEY?

11 In *It's A Wonderful Life*, George Bailey gets to see what life would be like without him. What he sees is not pleasant. He and the viewer realize just how many lives he touched, and how many lives would be different had he never been born.

Which brings us to this argument: Who is Minnesota's George Bailey?

What person impacted more lives of more athletes and nonathletes than anyone else in Minnesota history? Here's a hint: It's the same person who traded for Herschel Walker and hired Les Steckel.

That's right, Mike Lynn, former general manager of the Vikings.

That Walker trade alone impacted millions of lives. Besides the players involved in the trade, the Dallas Cowboys used draft picks acquired from the Vikings to assemble a Super Bowl team that touched the lives of every Cowboys fan, as well as players and fans of the teams the Cowboys beat.

Lynn's in-state impact also was wide-reaching. There was the Les Steckel hiring and the Les Steckel firing. There was bringing Bud Grant out of retirement for a season to replace

Steckel. There was hiring Jerry Burns to replace Grant. There were all the players Lynn acquired for Steckel, Grant, and Burns.

And then there's what Lynn did to the people of Minnesota when he pushed to get the Vikings out of Metropolitan Stadium in Bloomington and into the Metrodome in Minneapolis. You know what happened to the land where the old Met squatted? The Mall of America was plopped over it, and you can bet the mall has touched the lives—as well as the billfolds—of millions.

Lynn also crossed over to baseball and touched the lives of the Twins and their fans. He persuaded the Twins to move into the Metrodome. He also convinced the University of Minnesota to play its football games there.

As for the Vikings, Lynn put together a 10-person ownership group. There's a bunch of lives right there he George Baileyed.

One life in particular Lynn touched was Roger Headrick's. Headrick had been a business executive with no football experience. Lynn brought him in to be part of that ten-headed Vikings' ownership group. When Lynn decided to leave the Vikings and run the NFL's fledgling European league, Headrick replaced him. If there had been no Lynn, there would have been no Headrick, which means Denny Green never would have become the Vikings' coach. And if Green didn't become coach, then Mike Tice wouldn't have been around to replace him.

And if Tice hadn't been around to be fired by Zygi Wilf, who might not have been around if Lynn hadn't assembled the ownership group that sold the team to Red McCombs, who sold it to Wilf, then Brad Childress might not have become the Vikings' coach. Are you following all this? If so, then you also see that one life can touch so many others.

What George Bailey learned was that he made his hometown of Bedford Falls a far better place. Nobody is saying Mike Lynn made things in Minnesota far better than they'd been.

He just made them.

WAS DENNY GREEN A LOUSY COACH?

 There was nothing wrong with the way Denny Green coached in regular-season games. His game plans were solid. His teams won more often than not. He was a good coach . . . during the regular season.

It was a different story in the playoffs. Once in the postseason, he often appeared to suffer from the same malady as Tom Hanks' character in *Joe Versus the Volcano*: a brain cloud.

The bigger the game, the bigger the brain cloud.

You want proof of that diagnosis? We've mentioned this incident elsewhere in this book, but it's so terrible it's worth pointing out again.

After whisking through the 1998 regular season with a 15–1 record, the Vikings crushed the Arizona Cardinals by 20 points in their first playoff game. That put them in the NFC Championship Game against the Atlanta Falcons.

There should be a 1998 photo of Green in dictionaries next to the word lamebrain, because that is what he became in the final seconds of the 4th quarter.

With the score tied, and with 30 seconds left on the clock, the Vikings had a 3rd-and-3 from their own 27. Now, for some teams, that wouldn't be a good situation. But those 1998 Vikings had set an NFL scoring record with one of the most explosive and quick-hitting offenses the league had ever seen. Thirty seconds was a lot of time for an offense that had put up 556 points in the regular season.

But instead of taking a stab at getting a 1st down, Green had his quarterback, Randall Cunningham, take a knee and run out the clock. Green decided to take his chances in overtime. As it turned out, that was the wrong call. The Falcons kicked a field goal and won the game.

After the 2000 season, the Vikings were back in the NFC Championship Game. This time, the game wasn't won in over-time. It was won way earlier than that. The New York Giants routed the Vikings 41–0. No team had ever been beaten worse in an NFC title game. Kerry Collins, a mediocre quar-terback for much of his career, threw 5 touchdown passes against the Vikings.

It was the last time Green took the Vikings to a playoff

game. At the end of the next season, with one game yet to play, he quit as coach.

His regular-season record was 97–62, a .610 winning percentage. And that's good. But coaches aren't judged on what they do in the regular season. It's the postseason where they make their mark.

Denny Green's playoff record was 4–8. And that's lousy.

WHO WAS THE VIKINGS' BIGGEST DRAFT-DAY BUST?

13 Leo Hayden's NFL career can be condensed to two words: He sucked.

The Vikings pissed away the 24th overall pick of the 1971 draft on Hayden, a back who never once carried the ball for them. Hayden only lasted one season in purple. He spent the next two seasons with the Cardinals and ran for a whopping total of 11 yards.

He was the Vikings' biggest draft-day bust. That is, until Dimitrius Underwood came along.

Underwood wasn't just the Vikings' biggest draft-day bust. He was right up there among the NFL's all-time crappy picks.

Underwood was 6-foot-6, 312 pounds and even more of a looney toon than Daffy Duck.

In the first round of the 1999 draft, the Vikings used the 11th overall selection on quarterback Daunte Culpepper. Then they flushed the 29th pick of the first round down the commode by taking Underwood.

Did you ever forget to study for a big test when you were in school? That's sort of what the Vikings did when they chose Underwood. Vikings coach Denny Green and his underlings forgot to study up on him. They knew Underwood was a defensive end. They knew he played some decent football at Michigan State. If they had shoveled a bit deeper, they might have uncovered this nugget: His elevator didn't stop at every floor.

Just before the start of training camp, the Vikings signed Underwood to a five-year, $5.3 million contract. A five-minute contract would have been plenty long enough to cover his career with them.

Underwood took part in the morning practice on the first day of camp. He skipped out on the second practice of the day, never to be seen again by the Vikings.

The *Minneapolis Star Tribune* sent out a reporter to track Underwood down. The reporter located him in Philadelphia. Daffy, uh, Dimitrius said he was in conflict about whether to play football or become a full-time member of God's Squad and go into the ministry. Meanwhile, there also was a conflict over the bonus money the Vikings paid Underwood. The team had to wrangle with his agent to get most of it back.

Within a month, Underwood picked football over God and joined the Miami Dolphins. He—Underwood, not Him—

played in one preseason game.

He—again, Underwood—hurt his shoulder and, just a few weeks later, was found on a Lansing, Michigan, street, his neck bleeding from a self-inflicted knife wound.

A day earlier, Underwood had been thrown in jail for failing to pay child support. Somebody posted bail. Most people hightail it out of the hoosegow within nanoseconds of making bail. Not Underwood. He declined the chance to leave right away so he could spend time talking with another prisoner.

Clearly, Underwood had issues. And just as clearly, the Vikings didn't have a clue.

And that's how Dimitrius Underwood became their biggest ever draft-day bust.

WHO WAS MINNESOTA'S MOST UNDERRATED COACH?

14 Ever see the first few *Rocky* movies? Of course you did. You wouldn't be much of a sports fan if you didn't. Anyway, remember how Burgess Meredith played the role of Mick? He made him a crusty old crank with a gravel-soaked voice. You can just hear Mick telling Rocky, "You're gonna eat lightin' and you're gonna crap thunder!"

Now imagine Mick saying, "As long as I'm coach of the Vikings, Bob Schnelker will be my offensive coordinator!"

Anyone who knew Jerry Burns when he coached the Vikings could. Burnsie was a real-life Mick. He looked like him. He sounded like him. It was almost to the point where you'd swear Burgess Meredith met Burns somewhere along the way and patterned Mick after him.

If you knew Jerry Burns you didn't call him Jerry. You didn't call him Burns, either. He was Burnsie, and he was a character.

Burnsie had three hot buttons that could be pushed at any time. The mere mention of "killer instinct" was one of them. (Asking about Herschel Walker and whether there was a quarterback controversy brewing were the others.) The day after the Vikings backed into the NFL playoffs in 1987 because the St. Louis Cardinals lost, Burnsie went off on reporters because they said (a) the Vikings backed into the playoffs, and (b) the Vikings lacked killer instinct.

"Killer instinct, killer instinct," Burns ranted. "Whoever came up with killer instinct?"

When some smart-ass suggested it might have been Charles Manson, Burnsie said, "Yeah, Manson," and went back to his rant. He appeared to have no earthly idea who Charles Manson was.

Burnsie once ripped into the media and Vikings fans for criticizing Schnelker's play calling. He went on and on, his voice getting louder and angrier with each syllable. Finally, a reporter asked, "You won the game, didn't you?" Burns sure had, but you never would have known it from the way he carried on.

Don't get the wrong idea here. Burnsie wasn't just some hothead. He was, well, he was Mick come to life. He was charming in his own curmudgeonly way.

He also was one helluva coach, which often is forgotten by people who remember Burnsie's outbursts more than what he did on the sidelines.

Burnsie had been Bud Grant's offensive coordinator all those years the Vikings were winning division titles and going to Super Bowls. Bill Walsh is credited with being the originator of the West Coast offense, but Burnsie was running the same type of offense with the Vikings more than a decade before Walsh came along as the San Francisco 49ers coach.

Burnsie should have gotten the head coaching job after Bud Grant's first retirement following the 1983 season (which is what Grant wanted), but it was stupidly given to Les Steckel, who failed miserably and brought about Grant's return. Burnsie finally became the Vikings head coach in 1986, after Grant retired for a second time.

In 1987, Burnsie took the Vikings to the NFC Championship Game. It's a game the Vikings almost won, a game they might have won if Darrin Nelson hadn't thought an end zone pass intended for Anthony Carter was meant for him. But Nelson failed to make the catch, and the Vikings lost to the Washington Redskins 17–10. The Redskins went on to crush the Denver Broncos 42–10 in the Super Bowl. Had the Vikings beaten the Redskins, they would have been the ones routing the Broncos.

Burnsie was a character, that's for sure. Remembered more for his personality than for what he did on the field, Jerry Burns also was Minnesota's most underrated coach. That's even more for certain.

WHAT WAS THE DUMBEST THING A MINNESOTA COACH EVER DID THAT DIDN'T TAKE PLACE IN A GAME?

15

While he was coach of the Vikings, Mike Tice got caught scalping Super Bowl tickets. That was dumb.

But was it the dumbest thing a Minnesota coach ever did away from the game? Nah.

Clem Haskins' career as basketball coach at the University of Minnesota ended because some of his players cheated on their schoolwork. It was, by far, the most scandalous thing a Minnesota coach ever was involved in. But was it the dumbest thing a Minnesota coach ever did away from the game? Nah.

While coach of the Vikings, Denny Green laid out a blueprint in his autobiography of how he could go about overthrowing the team's owners.

In the final chapter of his 1997 book, *No Room for Crybabies*, Green threatened to sue members of the Vikings' then ten-person ownership group for trying to replace him with Lou Holtz. Green even included a letter he claimed he would send to the owners, who doubled as the franchise's board of directors.

The letter began, "Dear Directors: I am purchasing the 9% shares of the two individuals sitting in this room who contacted Lou Holtz , the former Notre Dame head coach, without authority last year and deliberately interfered with my ability to coach the team.... As a career coach of 26 years, who can be expected to coach for another 15 years, these two board members may have damaged my future career opportunities. In other words, I AM BUYING OR SUING."

He also included in the book a copy of the lawsuit he threatened he would file. After the book came out and writers pressed him about the threats, Green replied that he was just thinking out loud. Yeah, right. Now that's not just dumb. It's the dumbest off-the-field thing a Minnesota coach ever did.

Within a year of the book coming out, the Vikings were sold, but not to Green. Red McCombs purchased them.

In his first season with McCombs as owner, Green finished the regular season with a 15–1 record and took the Vikings to the NFC Championship Game, where he followed his dumb off-the-field move with some really dumb on-the-field decisions.

The Vikings became the first 15–1 team not to reach the Super Bowl. Green coached the Vikings another three seasons without getting to the Super Bowl. He never again threatened to sue for ownership of the team.

WHAT MINNESOTA ATHLETE FOUND THE MOST SUCCESS AFTER RETIRING FROM THE GAME?

16 When Bud Grant retired as an athlete, he became a massively successful football coach. He ranks right up there among Minnesota athletes who became successful after their playing careers ended.

But was he the most successful?

Uh, no.

A lot of athletes become coaches or managers once their playing days are over. It's a natural metamorphosis, almost like going from caterpillar to butterfly. That's what Ron Gardenhire did. That's what Jacques Lemaire did. Herb Brooks, Billy Martin, Tom Kelly, Norm Van Brocklin, Denny Green, and Mike Tice all did it, too.

You'd have a tough time finding a coach or manager who didn't once play the game.

Some athletes retire and go into the front office. Lou Nanne did that. So did Doug Risebrough and Kevin McHale, just to name a few.

But while athletes go from being athletes to coaches, managers, or front-office hotshots, they're still not leaving their sport. They are staying with something they know rather than venturing into an entirely different line of work.

That's really what we're after here, crowning the ex-athlete who hightailed it away from his or her sport to find overwhelming success.

And we're not talking about moving into the broadcast booth, either. Bert Blyleven, Jim Kaat, and Ahmad Rashad found success in TV and radio, but those jobs still involved sports.

We're talking about somebody like Fran Tarkenton, who hosted the television show *That's Incredible!*, became a computer software executive, and wrote books about business success. We're talking about somebody like Kent Hrbek, who started doing a successful TV show about the outdoors, or Paul Krause, who owned a golf course and was elected to Dakota County's board of county commissioners.

We're talking about Alan Page.

Of every athlete who ever played in Minnesota, nobody ever found more success after retirement from the game than Page.

Page was a Hall of Fame defensive tackle for the Vikings, one of the best ever to play his position. Now check this out: Page received his Juris Doctor from the University of Minnesota Law School while still playing for the Vikings. He became a practicing attorney with the law firm Lindquist & Vennum after his football career ended in 1981. (That's a good trivia question to hit Vikings fans with: Name the law firm Alan Page worked for after he retired from football.)

Anyway, Page was an associate with Lindquist & Vennum from 1979–84. In 1985, he became a Special Assistant Attorney General in the state's employment law division. After two years of doing that, he was made an Assistant Attorney General for the state.

And then in 1993, a little more than a decade after his playing days were over, Page became an Associate Justice on the Minnesota Supreme Court. He remained on the state's Supreme Court into the twenty-first century.

Page accomplished a great many things in football. Clearly, he accomplished great things after football, too.

DID MIKE TICE GET A FAIR SHOT?

Mike Tice never believed he did anything terribly wrong. He was simply scalping Super Bowl tickets. Plenty of other coaches were doing it. In 2005, he just happened to get caught.

That didn't help matters with his new boss, Vikings team owner Zygi Wilf, who kept talking about creating a culture of accountability and righteous living.

When several of Tice's players rented a couple of party boats, along with some strippers, and took a wild spin on Lake Minnetonka in October of that year, Tice had no idea what had gone on. He learned the sordid details about the same time the public did, which was when word leaked that those boats had been turned into a floating Sodom and Gomorrah. That night of alleged depravity, known as the Love Boat incident, didn't help matters with the new boss, either.

Wilf fired Tice within minutes of the final regular-season game in 2005. The Vikings won that game, beating the Chicago Bears 34–10 to finish with a 9–7 record. (Tice's four full seasons as the Vikings' head coach left him with a 33–34 overall record that included one win and one loss in the postseason.)

As the team's owner, Wilf can hire and fire whomever he wants, and for whatever reason.

However …

Wilf should have given Tice one more season.

Throughout his tenure as coach, Tice never was given much money to spend on free agents or assistant coaches. Red McCombs, the owner who preceded Wilf, was a tight-wad. When Tice was preparing for the 2005 season, McCombs still owned the team. He was so cheap he wouldn't even let Tice hire a new offensive coordinator after the old one, Scott Linehan, left. Why'd Linehan leave? The simple explanation: McCombs didn't want to pay him a fair wage.

Anyway, Tice had to make his offensive line coach pull double duty and also be the coordinator. Imagine getting into a boxing ring with an opponent and having your hands zip-tied behind your back. That's sort of what it was like for Tice in that final season.

Brad Childress, the coach who replaced Tice, was given the keys to the vault by Wilf and encouraged to spend whatever he felt necessary to bring a winning team to Minnesota.

Childress spent plenty. He brought in left guard Steve Hutchinson, an all-pro left guard with the Seattle Seahawks. He lured running back Chester Taylor away from the Baltimore Ravens and coaxed fullback Tony Richardson into leaving Kansas City after a long career with the Chiefs. Childress also went about upgrading the defensive secondary and adding depth along the offensive line. And he put together one of the largest coaching staffs in the NFL.

Still, it didn't make the Vikings any better. Based on their 2006 record of 6–10, they were quite a bit worse than Tice's financially undernourished 2005 team.

It would have been interesting to see what Tice could have done to improve that 9–7 team he had in 2005, if only Wilf had kept Tice and given him the carte blanche extended to Childress to sign players and assemble a staff.

If Tice failed, so be it. Then fire him. But at least he would have been given a fair shot.

WHAT WERE DENNY GREEN'S BEST LINES?

18 Denny Green had the most memorable meltdown of the 2006 NFL season after his Arizona Cardinals blew a 20–0 halftime lead and lost 24–23 to the Chicago Bears.

During a shrill rant that made it damn clear he was pissed off at his players for squandering the lead to a then-undefeated Bears team that didn't impress him all that much, Denny said, "The Bears are who we thought they were, and that's why we took the damn field! Now, if you want to crown them, then crown their ass! But they are who we thought they were, and we let them off the hook!"

Colorful as it was, that was one of Green's more coherent commentaries. People who remember Denny from his days as the Vikings' coach will recall that he often had a unique way of saying things.

Here, in descending order, are Green's best eleven lines from his time in Minnesota:

11.

"I'm a football coach. When you say 'play,' we play and we like it. It's called opportunity. Any time we get a chance to play, we play. We also know that to be world champions you've got to get into the playoffs. So, whenever they say 'play' if you can make it to the playoffs, then you are going to play."

10.

"You plan your work and work your plan."

9.

"We've got to win that first Super Bowl championship, be an organization that can win it all. I think once you do that, that's first. Then you take it to the next step."

8.

"You may be smiling, but other people are not smiling."

7.

"You've done nothing but denigrate me and the damn football team. So, now don't come to me all of a sudden and say that you care about the team."

6.

"There are people here who want to hear about the Tampa football game with the Minnesota Vikings. All right? Let them get done with that. And I want to finish answering the Tampa questions. Any other Tampa questions? . . . (Nearly thirty seconds pass with no questions.) . . . Any other questions on Minnesota and Tampa?"

5.

"My hand is on the plow and the best thing when your hand is on the plow is to look forward."

4.

"I'm always going to be on the high road. If you're looking for Denny Green . . . look on the high road. That's where I'll be."

3.

"There are two teams that wanted to win very, very badly. When that happens, only one can win."

2.

"Sometimes, you're gonna get to eat the dog. But sometimes the dog is gonna get to eat you."

1.

"Nobody can beat us when we play like we play when we play."

WHAT WAS THE BEST TRADE EVER BY A MINNESOTA TEAM?

19 The best trade ever? It's tough to argue with the Twins' trade that sent catcher A. J. Pierzynski to the San Francisco Giants for closer Joe Nathan and a couple of terrific young starting pitchers, Francisco Liriano and Boof Bonser.

But we will.

That Pierzynski trade may some day go down as the best swap a Minnesota team ever made, if the Twins reach the World Series with Nathan, Liriano, and Bonser playing key roles.

Nathan already has distinguished himself as one of baseball's elite closers, so it may not even take a World Series appearance for that trade to become the best ever. It could be enough if Bonser becomes a twenty-game winner and Liriano recovers from elbow surgery to battle teammate Johan Santana for Cy Young Awards.

Until something like that happens, though, the best trade of them all involved the Vikings, the New York Giants, and a quarterback by the name of Fran Tarkenton.

Tarkenton actually was the centerpiece of two trades between the Vikings and Giants.

In 1967, the Vikings swapped Tarkenton to the Giants for

first- and second-round draft choices in 1967, a first-round pick in 1968, and a second rounder in 1969. The Vikings used those picks to select running back Clinton Jones, wide receiver Bob Grim, offensive tackle Ron Yary, and guard Ed White.

Then, in 1972, Tarkenton was traded back to the Vikings for Grim, Norm Snead, Vince Clements, and first-round picks in 1972 and 1973.

A Viking once again, Tarkenton set NFL passing records and led the franchise to three Super Bowls with Yary and White anchoring the offensive line that blocked for him.

After his playing days were over, Tarkenton was inducted into the Pro Football Hall of Fame. Yary made it into the Hall of Fame as well. That meant two trades involving Tarkenton produced two Hall of Famers for the Vikings, meaning it will take a helluva lot to beat the trade that brought Tarkenton back to the Vikings.

WHAT WAS THE ODDEST THING A MINNESOTA ATHLETE DID (PRO DIVISION)?

20 In the fourth round of the 2003 draft, the Vikings picked a running back from Oregon named Onterrio Smith. Believing a young man with his talent should have been chosen much sooner, Smith immediately dubbed himself "The Steal of the Draft." Or, SOD for short.

Smith also had other nicknames for himself. When he showed up for his first training camp, he wanted to be called "The Entertainer." He already had been known as Big O, Little O, and just O, and he claimed fans gave him yet another nickname while at Oregon: Oh, Shitty.

"When I made a guy miss, they'd be like, 'Oh, shit,'" Smith once explained. And from that a "y" was added and yet another nickname was hatched. Smith liked that particular nickname so much he had "Oh, Shitty" put on his belt buckle.

He was a character, this Onterrio "Oh, Shitty" Smith.

He also was a troubled young man.

The reason Smith lasted until the fourth round of the draft was his history of drug and alcohol use and abuse. Smith began his college career at Tennessee, but that came to an abrupt end after he tested positive for marijuana. After he transferred to Oregon, he had a drunk-driving arrest while underage, and his license was suspended at the time.

Once he joined the Vikings, it was obvious Smith was loaded with skill. As a rookie, he was their second-leading rusher with 579 yards and, among the running backs, had a team-best 5.4-yard average per carry. In 2004, even though he served a four-game suspension for violating the league's substance abuse policy, Smith led the Vikings in rushing and was the leading receiver among backs.

By 2005, he was gone. He pissed away his career.

Ironically, his attempt to hide his own urine is what led to him pissing away his career.

While at Minneapolis-St. Paul International Airport on April 21, 2005, Smith was caught toting the "Original Whizzinator." Most law-abiding people didn't know there were knock-off Whizzinators, let alone the Original. If you had clean urine, chances are you had never heard of this contraption designed to beat drug tests.

It resembled a jock strap and was worn like one. There was a prosthetic penis attached to the faux jock strap, and the device came with accessories, including dried urine that was mixed with water to create the concoction used to beat drug tests.

Presumably, Smith was confident he had found a way to keep his dirty urine from being detected. Perhaps he should have been more concerned with the Original Whizzinator being detected. Smith became a national joke.

Instead of outsmarting the drug tests, Smith ruined his career. According to the *St. Paul Pioneer Press*, he "failed or missed a league-mandated drug test" in May 2005. A month later, the NFL suspended him for one year.

Mike Tice was the coach who drafted Smith and tried, unsuccessfully, to keep Smith on the straight and narrow. When Tice was fired after the 2005 season, it was pretty apparent Smith wouldn't be back with the Vikings. In April 2006, just before the latest NFL draft, the team terminated Smith's contract.

"We wish him well in his future endeavors," new Vikings coach Brad Childress said in a statement.

If Onterrio Smith's athletic future turns out anything like some of his past, you will be able to sum it up in two words:

Oh, shitty.

At least he'd still be able to wear the belt buckle.

WHO REALLY BUILT THE PURPLE PEOPLE EATERS?

21 It wasn't Bud Grant. He coached those teams, but he didn't assemble them. No, the architect of the Vikings teams that became known as the Purple People Eaters was Jim Finks.

As their general manager from 1964–73, Finks drafted and traded for the players that were the foundation of the Vikings' four Super Bowl teams.

Finks also hired Grant. They knew each other from the Canadian Football League. Finks had been a player, coach, and general manager with the Calgary Stampeders, giving him an up close view of Grant winning CFL championships with Winnipeg. So, when Norm Van Brocklin resigned as Vikings coach after the 1966 season, Finks plucked Grant out of Canada. Finks also brought Joe Kapp down from Calgary. Kapp, you may recall, was quarterback of the Vikings' first Super Bowl team.

A St. Louis lad born on the last day in August 1927, Finks went to the University of Tulsa and played quarterback and defensive back for the Pittsburgh Steelers from 1949–55. Back then, it was common for players to play both ways, something that gave Finks a firsthand understanding of what it took to play on offense and defense. He tapped into that knowledge when it came to putting together winning teams with the Vikings and, later, the Chicago Bears and New Orleans Saints.

Do you remember that great Bears team in the mid-1980s? As the Bears' general manager from 1974–82, Finks drafted 19 of the 22 starters on the team that beat New England in Super Bowl XX. He went from the Bears to baseball, becoming the Cubs' president and chief executive officer and overseeing a team that won the National League's Eastern Division title in 1984. After he left the Cubbies, Finks needed just two seasons to bring the Saints their first-ever winning team.

But before all that, he enriched the Vikings, lifting them from mediocrity to a franchise that became a dominant presence in the postseason.

In 1964, his first season with the Vikings, Finks drafted defensive end Carl Eller and acquired defensive tackle Gary Larsen. Eller and Larsen made up half of the Vikings' front four, which was the most celebrated and talented piece of the Purple People Eaters. Defensive end Jim Marshall already was with the Vikings when Finks arrived. In 1967, in what was one of the best drafts in Vikings history, Finks added defensive tackle Alan Page, who, along with Eller, would become Hall of Famers. That 1967 draft also yielded running back Clint Jones, wide receivers Gene Washington and Bob Grim, defensive back Bobby Bryant, and tight end John Beasley.

Finks also was responsible for trading Fran Tarkenton to the New York Giants in 1967 and for getting him back in 1972. As mentioned previously, Jones and Grim were selected with draft picks the Vikings received from the Giants in the first Tarkenton trade, as were tackle Ron Yary (1968) and guard Ed White (1969). Yary, the first overall pick of that 1968 draft, also is in the Hall of Fame.

That was some fine wheeling and dealing on Finks' part.

The Vikings won five division titles and went to two of their four Super Bowls under Finks' stewardship. But make no mistake: The Vikings went to all four of those Super Bowls because of the players Finks brought to Minnesota.

Finks resigned as the Vikings' executive vice president and general manager after the 1973 season following a dispute with the franchise's ownership.

In 1995, a year after his death at the age of 66 from lung cancer, Finks was inducted into the Pro Football Hall of Fame. It's the right place to be for the man who brought so much fame to the Vikings.

WHAT WAS THE VIKINGS' WORST DRAFT?

22 There's a garbage burning facility on the outskirts of Minneapolis. It emits quite a smell, but nothing emanating from that place can ever overtake the stench from the Vikings' worst draft in franchise history.

The three years the Vikings drafted following the Herschel Walker trade (1990–92) were bad. They didn't have a first-round pick, and they were without some second-round and later picks because of that dang Walker trade.

But even those drafts weren't as bad as the 1989 draft: The stinker of all Vikings drafts.

Vikings general manager Mike Lynn and his scouts were asleep at the switch during that draft. Either that, or they just threw darts at names and never hit the right name.

That 1989 draft was far worse than even the early years, when Bert Rose was the general manager and Norm Van Brocklin was coach. Even in those lean drafts, the Vikings came away with at least one player who would become a starter.

The Vikings' first three picks of the 1989 draft brought Wake Forest linebacker David Braxton, Brigham Young tackle John Hunter, and California tight end Darryl Ingram.

Braxton came in the second round. The Vikings didn't have a first-round pick that year. It had been swapped to Pittsburgh for linebacker Mike Merriweather.

Now, some people might argue that Merriweather should be considered when judging that 1989 draft because he was acquired for its first-round pick.

But the other picks were so miserable that the Vikings don't get any points for Merriweather. Besides, they gave up a first-round pick for a guy who sat out the entire 1988 season in a salary dispute. It's not wise to go swapping your top pick for a guy with rust on his bones. After being a three-time Pro Bowler with the Steelers, Merriweather had only a few bursts of achievement in four seasons with the Vikings. Most of the time, he was just average.

The players drafted in 1989 were quite a bit south of average. Braxton spent two undistinguished seasons with the Vikings, primarily as a special teamer. Hunter, the third-round pick, failed to make the team. Ingram, who came in the fourth round, lasted one season. Nobody else drafted made it out of training camp. It was only the third time in franchise history only two players in a draft made the regular-season roster. But at least those other times, in 1969 and 1971, the Vikings came away with players who became starters on their Super Bowl teams—guard Ed White (1969 draft) and safety Jeff Wright (1971).

If you're scoring (and if you are that's a scary thought), the others drafted in 1989 were Eastern Washington tackle Jeff

Mickel (6th round), Auburn nose tackle Benji Roland (7th round), Cal-State Fullerton defensive end Alex Stewart (8th round), Alabama State running back Brad Baxter (11th), James Madison linebacker Shawn Woodson (12th), and Ohio State wide receiver Everett Ross (also a 12th rounder).

Some Vikings fans are likely to have a recollection of Braxton or Ingram because they did spend time on the regular-season roster, but anyone who remembers Hunter or the others picked that year should take down those posters of ESPN draft guru Mel Kiper, Jr. and leave their mother's basement once in a while.

You've got to admit, that draft was daft.

WHO'S ON THE VIKINGS' ALL-TIME FANTASY TEAM?

23

There is one rule to be a member of this team: A player has to have shown a high level of consistency in multiple seasons with the Vikings.

That's why you won't see Daunte Culpepper as the quarterback, even though he had the best statistical season in Vikings history. During his career in purple, he was just too inconsistent.

We are going with a quarterback, two running backs, three wide receivers, a tight end, and a kicker. The third wide receiver is actually a swing player. It could have been a third running back but, over the years, the Vikings have had better wide receivers than running backs.

Anyway, here's the team . . .

QUARTERBACK

Fran Tarkenton. He's in the Hall of Fame, and he got there throwing mostly to decent-not-great wide receivers such as Gene Washington, John Gilliam, and Jim Lash. Tarkenton only had the better Ahmad Rashad as a receiver for his final three seasons. When he retired, Tarkenton was the NFL's all-time passing leader for completions (3,686), yards (47,003), and touchdowns (342). Just imagine the numbers he would have put up if he had our three fantasy wide receivers catching his passes.

WIDE RECEIVERS

Randy Moss, Cris Carter, and Anthony Carter. Moss and Cris Carter played together in the late 1990s and into the 21st century, and formed one of the most dangerous receiving tandems in league history. Cris Carter had 122 receptions in both 1994 and 1995, while Moss had seasons of 106 and 111 catches in 2002 and 2003, respectively. Cris Carter is the Vikings' career leader with 110 touchdowns, and Moss is second with 91. Both had 17-touchdown seasons. Cris Carter did it in 1995. Moss actually had seventeen touchdowns twice (1998 and 2003). Meanwhile, Anthony Carter was one of the league's best receivers in the 1980s, and had two of the Vikings' six-best receiving days with 184 yards in 1987 and 188 yards in 1988. He is third behind Moss (41) and Cris Carter (40) with twenty-two 100-yard receiving games for the Vikings. Only Cris Carter and Moss have more career touchdowns than Anthony Carter's 54 among Vikings wide receivers.

RUNNING BACKS

Chuck Foreman and Robert Smith. While Smith holds the Vikings' single-season rushing record with 1,521 yards in 2000, Foreman set the team single-game rushing record with

200 yards in 1976. Foreman was more productive in the red zone, scoring 75 career touchdowns from 1973–79. Smith had 38 career touchdowns from 1993–2000. Foreman holds the Vikings' record for most touchdowns in a season with 22—13 rushing, 9 passing—in 1975. Smith and Foreman rank first and second in overall rushing yardage for the Vikings.

TIGHT END

Steve Jordan. Jordan played in Minnesota from 1982–94. He is the pick because he was a reliable go-to guy on 3rd down and he leads all Vikings tight ends with 29 touchdowns.

KICKER

Gary Anderson. Even though he missed that 38 yarder that would have iced the 1998 NFC Championship Game for the Vikings, Anderson was otherwise dependable during his time with the team (1998–2002). Anderson had made 35 field goals in a row before that miss in the NFC title game, and he holds the NFL single-season record for points without a touchdown (164). He set the mark with those 35 field goals and 59 point-after kicks in 1998. He is second all-time in the NFL in career points behind Morten Andersen, who kicked for the Vikings in 2004 and surpassed Anderson's 2,434 points in December 2006 while kicking for the Atlanta Falcons.

This is a fantasy team, so just fantasize what kind of offense the Vikings would have had if members of this all-time team had played together.

WHO WAS THE VIKINGS' BEST OPEN-FIELD TACKLER?

24

You could make a case for Alan Page or Carl Eller as best open-field tackler. They're both in the Pro Football Hall of Fame. Page and Eller, though, did most of their best work at the line of scrimmage and in the backfield. Page, a tackle, and Eller, an end, made careers out of stuffing running backs and tormenting quarterbacks.

The same goes for other high-quality defensive linemen who played for the Vikings, such as Jim Marshall, Keith Millard, Chris Doleman, and John Randle.

All were exceptional tacklers, but in the open field none were the best the Vikings ever had.

Like Page and Eller, Paul Krause also is in the Hall of Fame. While he was a free safety, Krause wasn't known as all that great a tackler. Krause made it into pro football's shrine because he is the NFL's all-time interception leader with 81.

The Vikings' best tackler, statistically, was middle linebacker Scott Studwell, who played for the team from 1977–90. Studwell finished with 1,981 career tackles, 529 more than linebacker Matt Blair, the player with the second-most tackles in franchise history.

Studwell also holds team records for most tackles in a season (230) and in a game (24), and he leads the team in both solo tackles (1,308) and assisted tackles (673).

Studwell was a sure tackler, to be sure.

But he wasn't the Vikings' best open-field tackler. Most of Studwell's tackles were made in tight spaces. When backs tried running up the middle, they usually ran into Studwell. He wasn't known for his speed or lateral mobility.

Blair wasn't the best tackler in the open field, either.

Now, Joey Browner, he had speed. He had mobility. He was the Vikings' best open-field tackler.

A member of the Vikings from 1983–91, Browner was the Vikings' first-round draft pick in 1983 out of Southern Cal. The Vikings tried him first at cornerback, but soon realized he was better—much better—at strong safety. There, he could help out in the passing game and crunch ball carriers.

Vikings coach Jerry Burns always was marveling about how Browner had these incredibly strong hands and when he got a hold of someone, there was no getting away. Browner was into martial arts and claimed the leverage and hand-to-hand fighting skills he developed while earning a black belt helped him become a better tackler.

Burns made sure to put Browner on every punt and kick coverage team. Browner was the strong safety on defense, the safety net on special teams. If a returner got past everyone else, it was up to Browner to bring him down. Through 2006, Browner held the franchise record for most special teams tackles in a season with 38 in 1989.

Browner was named to six Pro Bowl teams (1985–90), made all-pro four times (1987–90), and was named to the 1980s All-Decade Team that was chosen by the Pro Football Hall of Fame.

His success was all because he could make the open-field tackle, and make it better than any Vikings player ever did.

WHO'S ON THE VIKINGS' ALL-TIME OFFENSE?

25 We previously went over the skill position players and the kicker when we named the Vikings' all-time fantasy team. If you haven't read it yet or have memory loss issues, here's a quick recap:

QUARTERBACK: Fran Tarkenton
WIDE RECEIVERS: Randy Moss, Cris Carter, and Anthony Carter
RUNNING BACKS: Chuck Foreman and Robert Smith
TIGHT END: Steve Jordan
KICKER: Gary Anderson

For this all-time offense, we're sticking with everyone just mentioned with one exception. We're going with just one running back and three wide receivers. Foreman makes the cut. Smith doesn't. The reason: Foreman was more of a dual threat. He could scald a defense running with the ball or catching it. He also was more dangerous near the goal line.

Anyway, now that you know the skill position players, here are the guys who would be blocking for them:

RIGHT TACKLE

Ron Yary. He's in the Pro Football Hall of Fame for the way he protected Tarkenton and opened holes for Foreman and other Vikings backs from 1968–81. Yary was named to six straight all-pro teams and seven Pro Bowls.

RIGHT GUARD

Ed White. He began his Vikings career at left guard, but was switched to right guard after six seasons. White and Yary made a terrific wall on the right side of the Vikings' line. White went to the Pro Bowl as a right guard in the final three of his nine seasons with the Vikings (1969–77).

CENTER

Mick Tingelhoff. He played in 270 straight games, never missing a start in his 17 seasons with the Vikings (1962–78). Tingelhoff played in eight straight Pro Bowls and was one of the league's dominant centers throughout his career. It's a travesty he's not in the Pro Football Hall of Fame.

LEFT GUARD

Randall McDaniel. He's the most athletic left guard ever to play in the NFL. Want proof? He could do a 360-degree spin in mid-air and dunk a basketball. Fast and strong, he played with the Vikings from 1988–99 and holds the team record for most Pro Bowl seasons (11). He's another guy who belongs in the Hall of Fame.

LEFT TACKLE

Gary Zimmerman. He and McDaniel protected the blind side of several Vikings quarterbacks better than any other tackle and guard ever could. Zimmerman went to four Pro Bowls during his seven seasons with the Vikings (1986–92) and was a Pro Football Hall of Fame finalist in 2007.

WHO'S ON THE VIKINGS' ALL-TIME DEFENSE?

26 Elsewhere in this book, we told you that the Vikings' best defensive tackle and end after Hall of Famers Alan Page and Carl Eller were Keith Millard and Chris Doleman. (Yeah, Jim Marshall and John Randle were gifted defensive ends, but Doleman was more of a threat to turn a quarterback into road kill.)

Now that we've established that, here's the Vikings' all-time defense, which includes Eller and Doleman at end and Page and Millard at tackle:

OUTSIDE LINEBACKERS

Matt Blair and Roy Winston. At most offensive positions and along their defensive line, the Vikings had players who could match up with the best players on other NFL teams. The Vikings never have been all that strong at outside linebacker, though. Blair gets one of the nods because of the versatility he showed while with the Vikings from 1974–85. Blair is the team's second all-time leading tackler and holds the team record for blocked kicks with 20. Winston gets the other nod because he was a reliable player for the Vikings (1962–76) and started in three of their four Super Bowls.

MIDDLE LINEBACKER

Scott Studwell. The Vikings' all-time leader in tackles, Studwell appeared to get better as he got older. He played for the Vikings from 1977–90, but didn't go to the Pro Bowl until 1987. He went back again the following season.

CORNERBACKS

Antoine Winfield and Carl Lee. Nobody from the Vikings' Super Bowl teams make the cut. The truth is, if the Vikings had corners who could cover better and make more tackles, they might have come away with at least one Super Bowl victory. Winfield, who joined the Vikings in 2004, continued to demonstrate through the 2006 season that he's the best cover/tackling cornerback in the league. Lee also was adept at covering receivers and making tackles for the Vikings from 1983–93. He made all-pro in 1988 and was selected to three Pro Bowl teams.

STRONG SAFETY

Joey Browner. As mentioned elsewhere in this book, Browner was the Vikings' best open-field tackler during his nine seasons with them (1983–91) and a member of the 1980s All-Decade Defense chosen by the Pro Football Hall of Fame.

FREE SAFETY

Paul Krause. The NFL's all-time leader in interceptions with 81, Krause was inducted into the Pro Football Hall of Fame in 1998. During his career with the Vikings (1968–79), he was their deep threat on defense. Vikings coach Bud Grant encouraged Krause to play deeper than other free safeties so he could be in position to pick off passes.

AROUND
TOWN

WHY WOULD YOU EVER ARGUE HOW MINNESOTA'S PROFESSIONAL TEAMS GOT THEIR NAMES?

27 The information you are about to peruse may come in handy some day to settle an argument or bet with a friend, relative, or fellow barfly. So, consider it a public service.

Here, in alphabetical order, is how the Timberwolves, Twins, Vikings, and Wild got their nicknames.

TIMBERWOLVES

On April 22, 1987, the NBA Board of Governors voted unanimously to expand the league by four teams. Franchises in Miami and Charlotte would join the league in time to play the 1988–89 season, while Minnesota and Orlando franchises would begin play in 1989–90. On September 17, 1998, the Minnesota franchise unveiled its logo for the Timberwolves. According to the team's press guide, "The nickname 'Timberwolves' was selected by a 2-to-1 margin over 'Polars' in a vote of 842 City Councils throughout the state."

TWINS

Fortunately for Minnesotans, Calvin Griffith wanted to sever ties with Washington when he moved the Senators to Minnesota in 1961. The Minnesota Senators wouldn't have made any sense, just as the Los Angeles Lakers and Utah Jazz still don't make sense. (When the Lakers left Minneapolis for Los Angeles, the nickname should have been left in the Land of 10,000 Lakes and not transferred to a city by an ocean. As for the Jazz, that nickname made perfect sense when the franchise was in New Orleans, but in Utah?) Anyway, calling the Twins the Twins was pretty much a no-brainer, seeing as how they would be playing in the Twin Cities.

VIKINGS

This comes straight from the Vikings' media guide, "In one of the first moves with the team, (in 1960 general manager) Bert Rose recommended the nickname 'Vikings' to the Board of Directors. The name was selected because it represented both an aggressive person with the will to win and the Nordic tradition in the northern Midwest." If you really want to impress friends, relatives, and fellow barflies with your knowledge of nicknames, ask them if they know how the Vikings also became known as the Purple People Eaters. If you get a blank look, tell them it was hijacked from the title of a 1958 song that became a No. 1 hit for six weeks for a fellow named Sheb Wooley. Now, if you really want to dazzle folks, ask them if they know the words to the song. Hit them with the first few lyrics: "Well I saw the thing comin' out of the sky; It had the one long horn, one big eye." And it goes on from there, as will we.

WILD

This explanation also comes straight from a media guide. According to the Wild guide, "On January 22, 1998, Minnesota and hockey fans all over the world were introduced to the Minnesota Wild. During a historic ceremony at Maplewood, Minnesota's Aldrich Arena, the organization revealed the name which was chosen from thousands of suggestions offered by Minnesota hockey fans over a six-month period." Apparently, Sheb Wooley's rendition of "The Happiest Squirrel in the Whole U.S.A." didn't translate well into a hockey-related nickname.

His version of "Fifteen Beers Ago" might make a pretty good anthem for barflies, though.

WHAT ARE THE THREE BEST SPORTS-RELATED MOVIES WITH A MINNESOTA CONNECTION, AND WHAT'S ONE GOOD PIECE OF TRIVIA FROM EACH MOVIE?

28 We'll go from the third-best movie to the best, and use some Hollywood lingo to start this off.

Roll 'em:

3. "LITTLE BIG LEAGUE"

A 12-year-old kid inherits a major league baseball team. That team is the Twins, which is the primary reason this 1994 movie makes the list. It's certainly not because of the cast, which includes Timothy Busfield, who also appeared in a supporting role in *Field of Dreams*.

It's not a terrible movie, but unless you're a demented fan who can't get enough of the Twins and anything associated with them, it will appeal more to children than adults.

The trivia question: Which former major league first baseman played a ball player in the movie? Answer: Leon Durham, who played for the St. Louis Cardinals, Chicago Cubs, and Cincinnati Reds from 1980–89 and finished his major league career with a batting average of .277 as well as 147 home runs and 530 RBI. Durham was playing for the St. Paul Saints when *Little Big League* was made. He was Leon Alexander in the movie.

2. "MIRACLE"

This was a damn good movie about the 1980 U.S. Olympic ice hockey team that shocked the Russians and the world by winning the gold medal. You don't have to be a hockey fan to like this movie. You just have to like a good tale about underdogs. Kurt Russell did a terrific impression of University of Minnesota hockey coach Herb Brooks in this 2004 film. His portrayal was much better than Karl Malden's depiction of Brooks in the 1981 movie *Miracle* on Ice. Russell had down the voice inflections and physical nuances of Brooks, who was a consultant on the film but died before its release.

The trivia question: Who portrayed his own father in the movie? Answer: Billy Schneider, son of Olympian Buzz Schneider. Buzz, a Grand Rapids native who played for Brooks at the University of Minnesota, was a left wing on the gold-medal winning U.S. team.

1. "FIELD OF DREAMS"

Yeah, the magical cornfield is in Iowa but Kevin Costner's and James Earl Jones' characters drove that beat up old VW bus to Chisholm, Minnesota, to track down Moonlight Graham, who was played by Burt Lancaster. One of the best goose-bump-inducing scenes in this 1989 movie takes place in Chisholm between Costner's Ray Kinsella and Lancaster's Dr. Archibald Graham. Graham says to Kinsella, "This is my most special place in all the world, Ray. Once a place touches you like this, the wind never blows so cold again. You feel for it, like it was your child." Here's another Graham quote that will make you goose-bumply: "Son, if I'd only gotten to be a doctor for five minutes, now that would have been a tragedy."

The trivia question: Who was that woman at the newspaper who read Doc Graham's obituary to Costner's and Jones' characters? Answer: Her name is Veda Ponikvar, and she started the *Chisholm Free Press and Tribune* in the late 1940s and served for half a century as writer, editor, and publisher.

WHAT MINNESOTA SPORTS VENUES HAVE FOOD THAT'S EDIBLE AND TASTY?

29

This isn't an argument that will offer food for thought. This is all about food for eating.

Anyone who attends a baseball or football game at the Metrodome, a basketball game at Target Center or Williams Arena, or a hockey game at Xcel Energy Center or Mariucci Arena knows that, if they're hungry, they're not going to find a gourmet meal at one of the concession stands.

Pretty much, they're going to find the basics: hot dogs, pizza, peanuts, popcorn, pretzels, ice cream, beer, and pop. (However, they won't find beer at Williams Arena or Mariucci Arena because they are on University of Minnesota grounds and the selling of alcoholic beverages is a campus no-no.)

There are other foods besides the ones just mentioned, if you check the concourses at the Dome and Twin Cities arenas. At the Metrodome, for instance, there are a few concession stands where you can buy a Subway sandwich or some barbecue from Famous Dave's. Most folks, though, stick with your basic snack and junk foods.

And that's what we're sticking with—the snacks and the junk.

Anyone new to ordering popcorn at the Metrodome should know that at times it is tasty, but not all the time. Sometimes, the popcorn at the Metrodome concession stands tastes like that stuff used to pack fragile items for shipping. What do they call them? Peanuts?

Speaking of peanuts, they are safe to order at just about any sporting venue. They're peanuts. You can't really screw them up, unlike pretzels.

When it comes to freshness, pretzels are a crapshoot at the Dome, Target Center, and Xcel. One game, the pretzels may be soft and chewy. The next game, it's like gnawing on jerky.

Freshness comes into play with hot dogs, too. Ever bite into a bun that tastes like it was made in 1953? That's always a possibility at a Twin Cities sports venue.

That said, the safest places for your taste buds are at Williams Arena or Mariucci Arena.

If you attend a Gophers basketball game (Williams) or a Gophers hockey game (Mariucci), you're usually in for a treat—a tasty treat.

The folks who run the concession stands at those University of Minnesota venues do a far better job of providing better and fresher snack and junk food than the pro venues.

Why? Maybe it's because beer can't be sold on campus, and the university's concessionaires realize people might be sober enough to actually care what the food they're eating tastes like.

WHAT ARE THE THREE BEST PLACES FOR BUDGET-MINDED PARENTS TO TAKE KIDS TO LEARN ABOUT MINNESOTA SPORTS?

30 Looking for an inexpensive way to educate the little ones about sports in Minnesota? Well, we've got three recommendations, and they're all places located in Minneapolis and St. Paul—you can visit all of them in the space of a few hours. And not a one of them charges an admission fee. We'll start in St. Paul.

HERB BROOKS STATUE

It's quite impressive, this statue of the legendary coach of the 1980 U.S. Olympic hockey team. Unveiled in February 2004, and located outside the east entrance to RiverCenter (which is attached to Xcel Energy Center, where the Wild play their games), the Brooks statue is made of bronze. It's a life-size tribute to a man who is larger-than-life to many Minnesotans. Frozen forever in 1980, the statue captures the moment the U.S. team beat Finland for the gold and shows Brooks with his arms raised. Doug Schiedel, a Minneapolis-based sculptor, depicted Brooks as he appeared in that moment: celebrating while wearing a plaid jacket and wing tips. When you take the kiddies to look at the statue, you can tell them about how Brooks led an underdog team of mostly college-age lads to the gold medal at the Lake Placid Olympics in 1980. And you can talk about how Brooks also coached the University of Minnesota to three NCAA national hockey titles in 1974, 1976, and 1979, and how hockey is such an important sport to many Minnesotans. And that just around the corner is where the Wild play against other NHL teams, and also where the high school hockey tournament is held. You also can get into how the Wild are Minnesota's second NHL team, and how they were preceded by the North Stars, and, well, you get the idea.

Then it's on to Minneapolis.

GEORGE MIKAN STATUE

Also life-size and also in bronze, the statue of the NBA's first great center is located in the lobby of Target Center, where the Timberwolves play their home games. The statue depicts Mikan taking a left-handed hook shot. You can start off by telling the kids about how Mikan led the Minneapolis Lakers to five league championships in the 1940s and 1950s and how he revolutionized the way big men played the game. You also should point out, particularly if you're with a child wearing glasses, that Mikan always wore thick glasses when he played, and it didn't stop him from achieving greatness. You then can tell the wee ones that the Lakers moved to Los Angeles in 1960 and that Minnesota was without an NBA team for several decades. After that, you can talk about the Timberwolves and how they also had a pretty impressive big man named Kevin Garnett. If they ask if he's also in bronze, tell them not yet, but maybe some day.

GOPHERS HALL OF TRADITIONS

The University of Minnesota football team was the No. 1 team in the nation six different seasons, and that's something you will find out when you visit this tribute to the Gophers. Located just through the main doors of the Gibson-Nagurski Football Complex on the Minnesota campus, the Hall of Traditions includes glass-enclosed photographs of coaches and players dating back to the earliest Gopher football teams in the 1880s. There also are trophies commemorating the school's six national championships, the last one coming in 1960, as well as the Heisman Trophy won by running back Bruce Smith in 1941. You and the kids also will find photos and information about the Gophers' 71st-team All America players, their 20 College Football Hall of Famers, their 18 Big Ten titles, their five Pro Football Hall of Famers, and their three Outland Trophy winners. You can start off talking about the Gophers and work your way to the Vikings and how both teams have shared the same stadium, the Metrodome, for a quarter of a century.

And then your tour is done.

Total cost: Maybe a couple bucks in gas and parking meters.

Value put on spending quality time with the kids: Priceless.

WHAT ARE THE BEST BITS OF MINNESOTA SPORTS TRIVIA YOU'VE NEVER HEARD?

31

If you're reading this book, chances are you know something about Minnesota sports, maybe even a lot of things. Well, here are ten things you may not have known.

10.

The movie *Miracle* played it loose with the facts. Oh, the movie got it right about the 1980 U.S. Olympic hockey team winning the gold medal. But there were many inaccuracies, including one involving former North Stars executive Lou Nanne. In the movie, the actor portraying Nanne says of Mike

Eruzione, "Cross him off the list. The kid doesn't stand a shot in hell of making the team." Eruzione became team captain and scored the goal that beat the Soviets in the game that prompted Al Michaels' immortal "Do you believe in miracles?" line. As for the real-life Nanne, he said the movie "took a lot of license" and that he "never said that about Eruzione. I didn't have any say who was on the team."

9.

Christian Laettner had a reputation for not always showering after playing games for the Timberwolves.

8.

When Mike Tice became the Vikings' head coach in 2001, he said Daunte Culpepper needed to become a student of the game. That season, Culpepper took a laptop computer home to watch DVDs of games. When Tice checked the computer, he saw that Culpepper had been watching DVD movies.

7.

Teammates used to call Vikings linebacker Jesse Solomon "Early Man," cruelly joking that they believed he resembled man in his early stages of evolution.

6.

In the early 1990s, a local TV reporter attempted to date the star player on each of Minnesota's professional sports teams.

79

5.

Mike Tice once asked reporters for advice on discipline. He wanted to know whether they believed he should suspend Randy Moss for misbehaving, explaining he wanted to collect as many opinions as possible.

4.

Despite his outgoing public persona and the perception he and Kent Hrbek were close, Kirby Puckett never socialized with Hrbek once they left the clubhouse.

3.

Doug Martin's nickname was "Big Blood" when he was a defensive end with the Vikings, but it had nothing to do with having large corpuscles.

2.

In 1987, Kirby Puckett had a date with a woman just before going 6-for-6 with 2 home runs against the Milwaukee Brewers. Before the 1991 World Series, for luck, Puckett approached the woman about having another date. Now married, she declined.

1.

The Love Boat incident in 2005 wasn't the first time members of the Vikings had more than Xs and Os on their minds. In the 1980s, there was the Squeals on Wheels incident. It involved several members of the Vikings who, during training camp in Mankato, hired a dancer to do more than dance in a rented R.V.

SHOULD MINNESOTA'S NATIVE AMERICANS PUT CASINO MONEY TOWARD STADIUMS?

32

They're a sovereign nation, so what they earn they should keep. After being oppressed and impoverished for years, they shouldn't have to share. They should be left alone.

Those are just a couple of reasons some people will give for why Native American tribes that run casinos in Minnesota shouldn't have to spread the wealth with non-tribal members.

It is considered politically incorrect to suggest that these casinos contribute even a fraction of their money pile to anyone outside the tribe.

Well, OK. We'll be politically incorrect. The tribes should share their casino money with the state. Other businesses in Minnesota have to cough up money to the state. And everyone else in the state has to pay taxes, whether it's property taxes, income taxes, or a sales tax. There shouldn't be exceptions. Native American casinos should have to pay something.

We're not talking about a bulk of the money here. To paraphrase Don Fanucci in *The Godfather, Part II*, the Native Americans should give the state just enough to wet its beak. In other words, just enough to help subsidize some of those sports stadiums and arenas professional and college teams are always trying to get built with taxpayer dollars.

The money would have to be earmarked for public facilities. To get the cultural and artsy crowd behind this idea, that also would mean casino money going toward the renovation and construction of theaters and museums.

But mostly, it'd be for stadiums.

Why should the people who buy goods in Hennepin County have to bear the brunt of the cost of a new Twins stadium in Minneapolis, just because the city lies within Hennepin County? That Twins stadium will be funded by a $0.15 sales tax, which comes out to a $0.03 surcharge on every $20 spent in Hennepin County. But everyone in the state can enjoy the stadium—why not spread out the cost? How about a small surcharge on every $20 earned by these American Indian casinos?

Or how about this: Every casino is on Native American land. But to access the casinos, people must drive on public roads. So, at the very end of these public roads, just before the Native American-owned roads begin, the state should put up toll booths.

Yep, charge the people who want to get to the casinos. The toll booths can even be made to look like slot machines. It'd be another revenue source for the state, and help get people in the mood to gamble, too.

All right, maybe nobody will get behind either of these ideas. But some way, somehow, these Native American casinos should have to contribute to the state coffers and help get stadiums built and museums and theaters renovated.

But mostly, it'd be for stadiums.

WHAT IF SOME THINGS THAT HAPPENED NEVER HAPPENED?

Here are six what-if scenarios related to Minnesota sports:

WHAT IF NORM GREEN HADN'T MOVED THE NORTH STARS?

Had they stayed, the North Stars likely would have moved into Target Center. There would be no Wild. There would be no Xcel Energy Center. There might have been a Stanley Cup championship for the North Stars, though. North Stars coach Bob Gainey became the team's general manager in Dallas and assembled a team that won the Stanley Cup in 1999. He may have done the same thing had the North Stars stayed put.

WHAT IF GARY ANDERSON HAD MADE THAT FIELD GOAL IN THE 1998 NFC CHAMPIONSHIP GAME?

Anderson had converted every field goal he attempted during the 1998 season, right up until he missed that 38 yarder. Had he made that kick with just over two minutes to play, the Vikings would have had a 10-point lead and likely beaten the Atlanta Falcons. Instead, the Falcons won in overtime with a 38-yard field goal of their own. If the Vikings had won, they would have faced the Denver Broncos in the Super Bowl, and probably lost. Instead, the Broncos crushed the Falcons 34–19 in Super Bowl XXXIII.

WHAT IF THE TIMBERWOLVES HAD TRADED FOR ALLEN IVERSON?

The Timberwolves were interested in acquiring Iverson from the Philadelphia 76ers during the 2006–07 season, but the Denver Nuggets came up with a better offer. Had Iverson been teamed up with Kevin Garnett, the Timberwolves would have had two of the NBA's best basketball players on the floor together and might have won their first league title. Or, Iverson and Garnett could have bickered over whose team it was, and team chemistry would have been destroyed.

WHAT IF THE GOPHERS' CHEATING SCANDAL HAD NEVER BEEN UNCOVERED?

Clem Haskins might still be coaching the men's basketball

team at Minnesota. He would only be 64 at the start of the 2007–08 season. When the academic cheating scandal was revealed by the *St. Paul Pioneer Press* in March 1999, the Gophers were on their way to becoming a fixture in the NCAA tournament. It's altogether possible Haskins would have had the Gophers among the top-ranked teams in the country on an annual basis, and might have even led them to a national championship.

WHAT IF ARMEN TERZIAN OR ANOTHER OFFICIAL HAD THROWN A FLAG?

As mentioned elsewhere in this book, to this day, Vikings fans believe a penalty should have been called on Dallas Cowboys receiver Drew Pearson for shoving Nate Wright in the final seconds of an NFC playoff game in 1975. Instead, Pearson's Hail Mary touchdown catch won the game. Terzian was hit in the head with a whiskey bottle by an angry fan because he didn't throw a flag. If Terzian or any other official had thrown a flag, the Vikings would have won the game and might have gone on to win their first Super Bowl. That 1975 team was Bud Grant's best.

WHAT IF KIRBY PUCKETT DIDN'T MAKE HIS LEGENDARY LEAPING CATCH IN GAME 6 OF THE 1991 WORLD SERIES?

Ron Gant would have had a 3rd-inning home run and it's unlikely the game would have gone into extra innings, which means Puckett couldn't have won the game with a home run in the 11th inning. Therefore, there would not have been a Game 7. The Atlanta Braves would have won the 1991 World Series in six games.

WHO IS MINNESOTA'S MOST POPULAR SPORTS ARTIST?

34 Actually, we can narrow it down even more than that and ask, "Who's the Twin Cities' most popular sports artist?"

St. Paul and Minneapolis are the birthplaces of two of America's greatest artists—LeRoy Neiman (St. Paul) and Charles Schulz (Minneapolis).

While born west of the Mississippi in 1922, Schulz grew up just east of it in St. Paul. He died in February 2000 from cancer at age 77 after becoming internationally known for his comic strip work.

Neiman, who was born in 1927, gained worldwide fame as a sports artist for illustrations related to football, baseball, basketball, hockey, boxing, golf, skiing, horse racing, tennis, and track and field. He was even the official artist for five Olympics.

Neiman has a distinct style. Considered an American

Impressionist, he uses brilliant strokes of color to create art that has wide appeal.

But does it appeal to little kids? Maybe, but not nearly as much as Schulz's art does.

And Schulz's art has even wider appeal than Neiman's, because anyone from a toddler to an octogenarian, or older, enjoys his work.

That's why Schulz beats out Neiman as Minnesota's best sports artist. Okay, Schulz was a cartoonist who created the "Peanuts" comic strip but, hey, that's art, too.

Who doesn't get a kick out of watching Lucy pull the football away from Charlie Brown just as he's about to kick it? You can see it a thousand times and it never gets tired or old. Part of the enduring charm of Charlie Brown was that he wasn't any good at sports, but he kept at it just the same. And millions of people, people here in Minnesota and around the globe, kept going back to see what act of athletic failure would happen next. Besides football, Schulz worked baseball, ice hockey, and other sports into his "Peanuts" strip.

Schulz got people of every age to care about those lines he drew on paper. They came to life, and they live on in memories as well as in syndication.

To paraphrase a line from "Peanuts," you were a good man, Charles Schulz. And, even in death, you are Minnesota's most popular sports artist.

WHAT MEDIA PERSONALITY IMPACTED MINNESOTA SPORTS MORE THAN ANYONE ELSE?

35 Minnesota used to be a safe place for coaches and athletes. A coach could be doing a lousy job and members of the media would be lined up to kiss his ass. It was the same thing with athletes. If a quarterback threw three interceptions in a game, or a pitcher got tattooed for five runs in an inning, there wouldn't be media criticism. There would be excuses offered on the player's behalf. The Minnesota media was a warm and cuddly bunch.

That is, until the 1980s.

The media became more cynical and more critical during that decade, and the leading cynic and critic was Tom Barnard, host of the KQRS Morning Show. That radio show happened to be the highest-rated morning show in America, according to the station literature. And, starting in the late 1980s and right on into the twenty-first century, Barnard offered listeners wit and wicked shots at coaches and athletes.

Early on, Barnard and program director Dave Hamilton

decided that athletes were fair game for skewering. They cracked open the door, making it easier for other radio shows and newspapers to come down harder on athletes, coaches, and team executives than ever before.

One of the first athletes Barnard scalded was Twins pitcher George Frazier. Everyone knew Frazier had no talent, but Barnard was the first to come right out and say it. He criticized Twins catcher Tim Laudner's speed and challenged him to a footrace. He tore into another Twins pitcher, Shane Rawley, for describing himself as a "Renaissance Man."

Barnard had no use for Timberwolves guard J.R. Rider, saying he would go watch Rider play when "sparks flew out his ass." Sparks never flew, and Barnard never watched Rider play.

On his show, Barnard often ran satirical bits poking fun at coaches and players who took themselves far too seriously. Back when Kirby Puckett had a pristine public image, Barnard was doing Puckett bits that included a sound effect suggesting that Puck was masturbating. Barnard didn't believe anyone could be as perfect as Puckett was portrayed, and it turned out he was right. Puckett's wife called the station pleading that the bits be stopped.

Vikings running back Darrin Nelson called the station himself, asking that Barnard stop running a bit that made fun of Nelson's high-pitched voice. Former Vikings punter Greg Coleman complained after Barnard repeatedly called him Gandhi because, well, Coleman had a shaved head and there was a resemblance to the ol' Mahatma.

89

Denny Green never called, but he allegedly seethed over bits that made fun of his weight and alleged dalliances with women.

There also were bits ripping Vikings coach Mike Tice for being a blockhead, and Vikings owner Red McCombs for being an even bigger blockhead than Tice. And then there were the "Burnsie Bedtime Stories." These were hilarious bits in which TV news anchor Jeff Passolt, a member of the KQRS Morning Show, would imitate Vikings coach Jerry Burns' voice and the way he sprinkled curse words into just about every sentence. The bits were what they suggested—about Burnsie telling bedtime stories to young children. Burnsie's own children loved the bits so much they requested copies of them.

Not every relative of a coach or athlete tweaked by Barnard loved it. But a lot of them listened to him every morning. They wanted to hear what was being said by the media personality who impacted Minnesota sports more than anyone else.

(Author's note—Fair Disclosure—I have listened to and bantered with Barnard every morning for nearly twenty seasons as a member of the KQRS Morning Show. But no, I'm not pimping Barnard because I've worked with him. I'm giving him his props because coaches and athletes have told me Tom's tweaking and critiquing has had more effect than anyone else in the Minnesota media over the past two decades.)

BASEBALL

WHICH OF THE TWINS' WORLD SERIES CHAMPIONSHIPS WAS MOST SPECIAL?

36 There's no crying in baseball.

It's a catchy movie line, but come on. We all know the truth. Of course, there's crying in baseball.

You can bet Fred Merkle cried or, at the very least, winced the day he got tagged with the nickname "Bonehead." How about Mordecai "Three Finger" Brown? You don't think he cried out in pain when he lost part of his index finger in a farming accident? And you just know Babe Ruth got weepy on those days when his favorite vendor at Yankee Stadium ran out of hot dogs.

In October 1987, there was plenty of crying in Minnesota. It was about baseball, specifically the Minnesota Twins winning the World Series. There were cries of disbelief, of joy, and of run-on words such as "Ohmygodohmygodohmygod!" For cryin' out loud, there were thousands of people crying out loud.

Kirby Puckett, Kent Hrbek, Gary Gaetti, Frank Viola, Bert Blyleven, and the rest of that outfit made it a magical October . . . especially at the Metrodome.

Over the years, people would whine about the Metrodome being a lousy place to watch a baseball game. They were right. But nobody was complaining in 1987 when the Twins won every postseason game played there, including four in the World Series, to beat the St. Louis Cardinals 4–3.

Though miserable on the road in 1987—they were 29–52 away from home during the regular season—the Twins became a wondrous bunch once they got under the Metrodome's Teflon sky. In Game 1 at the Dome, left fielder Dan Gladden had 5 RBI and Frank Viola allowed just 5 hits over 8 innings. Voila, the Twins won 10–1. Game 2 also was at the Dome. The Twins scored 6 runs in the 4th inning and put away the Cards 8–4.

Then it was on to St. Louis, and three losses. No problem for the Minnesota lads. They returned for what folks around Minnesota fondly call Dome cooking. In Game 6, the Cardinals had a 5–2 lead in the top of the 5th. In the bottom of the 5th, it was a different story. The Twins scored 4 runs. They added another 4 in the bottom of the 6th on Hrbek's grand slam. Puckett went 4-for-4 in the game, and scored 4 runs.

And then it was on to Game 7, and into history. Once again, the Cardinals took the lead. And, once again, the lead fizzled. Viola ended the 1987 Series the way he started it—with a dominating performance. The Twins won 4–2, becoming the first team to capture the World Series by winning all four games at home.

If you trace back through the Twins' family tree, you will find the 1924 Washington Nationals, who won the World

Series. The Nationals became the Senators, who became the Twins when Calvin Griffith shifted the franchise to Minnesota in 1961. But the people of Minnesota don't care that the Nationals won in 1924. That was ancient history . . . another time, another place.

This 1987 victory, though, belonged to Minnesota. It was the first championship by a professional team in the Land of 10,000 Lakes since the 1953–54 Minneapolis Lakers won the NBA title.

The 1991 Twins won a terrific seven-game World Series over the Atlanta Braves, and that certainly was special. You had Puckett's awesome catch in Game 6, and his home run to force a seventh game. And what Jack Morris did in Game 7 was a work of frickin' art.

People were thrilled, to be sure.

But . . .

In 1987, it was the Twins' first World Series title. And whether it's a beer on a hot and muggy day or the birth of a child or a world championship by your favorite baseball team, there's always something just a little bit more special about that very first one.

And in 1987, what the Twins did was enough to make Minnesotans cry into their Homer Hankies.

WHO WAS MORE IMPRESSIVE IN THE 1991 WORLD SERIES: KIRBY PUCKETT IN GAME 6 OR JACK MORRIS IN GAME 7?

37

Kir-BEEEEEEE PUCK-it!

There was nothing like it; nothing like the way Bob Casey would say Kirby Puckett's name over the Metrodome's P.A. system.

And there was nobody like Puckett; not before, not since.

This 5-foot, 8-inch outfielder from the Chicago projects enchanted the people of Minnesota. He was cuddly and popular; a teddy bear come to life.

This teddy bear of a man could hit and field and sling an entire team on his back and carry it to places it had never been, like a World Series championship.

He did that twice. In 1987, he led the Twins to their first World Series title. That was the World Series that introduced Puckett to the nation.

In 1991, he reintroduced himself in a big way.

The Twins were back in the World Series and Puckett was

back being a hero, particularly in Game 6.

He didn't win the game singlehandedly over the Atlanta Braves. It just seemed that way.

Trailing 3–2 in the best-of-seven shindig, Puckett pretty much told his teammates he would make sure there would be a Game 7 by leading them to victory in Game 6. He wasn't boasting. He was just telling it like it would be. In the 3rd inning of that sixth game of the 1991 World Series, Puckett made a leaping catch over the plexiglass wall in left center to hijack a home run from Ron Gant. He then won the game in the 11th inning with a home run off Charlie Leibrandt that landed in the left-center seats. Puckett circled the bases pumping his fist as people all around the Metrodome squealed and hugged. It was a Kodak, Canon, and Nikon moment.

Oh, Puckett also stole a base in the game, scored twice, and finished with 3 RBI, all while going 3-for-4.

He was magnificent.

However . . .

Jack Morris was even more magnificent.

What Puckett did in Game 6 was awesome. What Morris did in Game 7 was epic.

Some folks will claim that without what Puck did in Game 6, there's no Game 7. Well, without what Morris did in Game 7, maybe there's no second World Series trophy for the Twins.

Michelangelo with a chisel in his hand in the sixteenth century was no more impressive than Morris with a baseball in his hand on an October night in the late twentieth century.

Morris went 10 innings—10 innings that'll send you to a thesaurus searching for the right word to describe his performance: spectacular, incredible, astounding, marvelous, stupendous, or simply wow.

Nah, words just don't do it justice.

Manager Tom Kelly tried to take Morris out of the game an inning earlier, but Morris basically told him to get lost. You couldn't pry him off the mound with a crowbar. This was his night, his game. He wasn't giving an inch, or a run.

The Twins scored the game's only run when Gene Larkin's pinch hit in the bottom of the 10th scored Dan Gladden. Larkin's hit ended the game and the World Series, but Morris's pitching is what won it.

Morris grew up in St. Paul, but spent most of his baseball career in Detroit with the Tigers. He was thirty-seven when he finally got back to Minnesota to play some ball. He lasted just one season with the Twins, that 1991 season.

He made it a season nobody will forget because he made it a Game 7 nobody will forget.

WHICH PROFESSIONAL MINNESOTA ATHLETE SHOULD A GAL WANT TO BRING HOME TO MEET THE FOLKS?

38 Ben Stiller's character in the movie Meet the Parents had a tough time kissing up to his girlfriend's mother and father, particularly the father. It's like that in a lot of relationships, mainly because parents are protective of their children. They're even more protective of their daughters. No mom or dad prays nightly that their little girl will bring home a drunk, a drug addict, or an ex-con and say, "Mom, Dad, we're in love. I hope you can overlook his faults."

And there are plenty of professional athletes with plenty of faults: DWI arrests, drug abuse, steroid use, assault, gun play, and various acts of violence. When you mix youth, wealth, and fame, it can be a dangerous sociological cocktail. (See the arrests and/or court appearances of the likes of Randy Moss, Keith Millard, Koren Robinson, Fred Smoot, and Eddie Griffin for details.)

Some athletes can handle the money and fame that comes

their way, and behave in a mature manner. And some take a cruise on the Love Boat.

University of Minnesota men's hockey coach Don Lucia once said he was "a goody two shoes" growing up. A goody two shoes; that's the kind of guy sane parents want their daughters to bring home.

They're out there. A gal has just got to look. And she has to look extra hard when she gets into a relationship with an athlete. It's too easy to get caught up in the money and fame of an athlete, and look past the warts. But the ideal athlete/beau should come equipped with several qualities. He should be courteous, respectful, loving, and, of course, loaded with talent.

Let's be honest here. If you're a parent, it's great if your daughter is dating an athlete who is courteous, respectful, and loving. It's even greater when he's loaded with talent. It means he has the kind of earning power that is going to get him a long-term, big bucks contract and ensure your baby girl is set for life, should they end up at the altar.

The kind of athlete we're talking about is, well, he's kind of like Twins catcher Joe Mauer.

Any father in Minnesota would bust his buttons with pride if his daughter walked in the door with somebody like Mauer.

Besides being one of the best catchers in baseball, Mauer is one of the best catches out there. He comes with all the desirable traits: manners, looks, talent. We're talking Triple Crown winner here.

If you live in Minnesota and have a daughter, who could be

a better dating prospect than a Minnesota-born pro athlete who is well-behaved, has tremendous earning potential, and lists his mother's lasagna as his favorite food?

Guys like Mauer usually aren't on the market for long, though. During the 2006 season, when he won the American League's batting title, Mauer was dating 2005 Miss USA Chelsea Cooley.

If somebody like Mauer is unavailable, a Justin Morneau type also would do just fine. Morneau was Mauer's teammate and roommate during the 2006 baseball season. He's got a lot of the same fine attributes as Mauer. Plus, Morneau grew up playing hockey in his native Canada, which would be a huge bonus for a lot of Minnesota moms and dads fond of baseball and hockey.

No parents could complain if their daughter came home with a young Alan Page clone, either. Not only was Page one of the NFL's best defensive tackles, he also was a high achiever off the field and became a Minnesota Supreme Court justice.

If you have a daughter, it's unlikely she will come strolling in with a Joe Mauer, a Justin Morneau, or a young Alan Page on her arm.

But you can dream, can't you?

WHAT'S A BIGGER TRAVESTY, THE BASEBALL HALL OF FAME WITHOUT BERT BLYLEVEN OR WITHOUT JACK MORRIS?

39 First, let's get something straight. Bert Blyleven and Jack Morris both belong in baseball's Hall of Fame.

The knotheads who vote for the Hall of Fame have been blowing it for years. Well, OK, not all of them are knotheads; just those who haven't supported Blyleven and Morris.

To vote, you have to be a ten-year member of the Baseball Writers' Association of America. A lot of these writers are self-anointed protectors of the Hall of Fame, taking it upon themselves to make sure the club stays exclusive. And that's the problem. Some are stingy with their vote simply because they can be. Some won't vote for more than a player or two a year, though they can vote for up to ten. Some won't vote for a player in his first year of eligibility no matter who he is or what he did.

Did you know Babe Ruth wasn't a unanimous pick for the Hall of Fame? Nor was Ty Cobb or Cy Young. Heck, Cy Young didn't even get into the Hall of Fame the first year it existed in 1936; Cobb, Ruth, Honus Wagner, Christy Mathewson, and Walter Johnson were the ones who made it in that first year. Young went into the Hall in 1937, along with other first-year snubs Nap Lajoie and Tris Speaker.

In the history of Hall of Fame voting, nobody has ever received unanimous support. (For election, a ball player needs to be chosen on 75 percent of the ballots.) Check this out: Rogers Hornsby received votes in five Hall of Fame elections before getting in. And he won 7 batting titles and had a career batting average of .359, highest ever in the National League.

Hornsby had to overcome what Blyleven and Morris have yet to overcome, and what they may never be able to: persnickety voters.

Blyleven won 287 games in 22 seasons, and had a career ERA of 3.31. He led the American League in shutouts three times and, after the 2006 baseball season, ranked 5th all-time in strikeouts, 9th in starts, 9th in shutouts, and 25th in wins.

Morris pitched 18 seasons, won 254 games, and had a career ERA of 3.90.

He pitched on three World Series championship teams— the 1984 Tigers, the 1991 Twins, and the 1992 Blue Jays— and his performance in Game 7 of the 1991 Series was one for the ages. Morris also had three 20-win seasons, three 200-strikeout seasons, and, after the 2006 season, ranked

31st all-time in strikeouts and was tied for 39th in wins.

His exclusion from the Hall of Fame is an ever bigger travesty than Blyleven's.

While Blyleven ranks higher in several statistical categories, Morris was the more dominant pitcher in his era. Morris played four fewer seasons than Blyleven, yet had more 20-win seasons (3 to 1). Morris tied for the American League lead in wins twice, something Blyleven never did. Jack also had a better winning percentage than Bert, and he received Cy Young Award votes seven times, compared to Blyleven's four. But this isn't meant to be a knock against Bert Blyleven.

They both belong in the Hall of Fame.

WAS KIRBY PUCKETT A GREAT GUY?

40 Kirby Puckett was a great baseball player. Anyone who says otherwise is loopy.

Fans loved Puck: that hustle, that smile, those kinds of things made him likable. Plus, he didn't have one of those chiseled bodies you see in underwear ads. He was stocky. He was shorter than most pro athletes. He looked like normal people look.

But he sure didn't play ball like normal people. He had an inner mechanism that could lift his game. Take Puck out of the 1987 and 1991 World Series and not only do the Twins fail to win their championships, they don't even make the playoffs. He was that good, that great a ball player.

He did some fine things in the community, too. His annual celebrity pool tournament raised millions for charity. In 1993, he received the Branch Rickey Award for service to his community. Also in 1993, in a reader survey by Baseball America, Puckett was voted Baseball's Best Role Model and Friendliest Player. In 1996, he won the Roberto Clemente Man of the Year Award.

But there was another side to Puckett, a Darth Vader side.

The first smudge on his reputation came in December 2001, when his wife, Tonya, told police in Edina, where they lived, that Puckett had a history of violent behavior. She told the *St. Paul Pioneer Press* she went to police after claiming Puckett said in a phone conversation that he "was going to kill me."

She also claimed Puckett once tried to strangle her with an electrical cord, and that he put a cocked gun to her head while she held their two-year-old daughter, and that he used a power saw to slice through a door.

When word of Tonya's allegations reached the public, some people believed it. Some didn't. They couldn't fathom Puck, that lovable and huggable Puck, ever doing such vile things.

Tonya also said she learned from a private investigator she hired that her husband had a slew of girlfriends. One of the girlfriends told the *Pioneer Press* she and Puckett began an 18-year affair before Kirby ever met Tonya. That woman also claimed that after years of begging Puckett for birthday and Christmas presents, he gave her a vibrator.

Kirby and Tonya separated, then divorced.

The Twins had been paying Puckett $500,000 a year to be little more than a goodwill ambassador. That job disappeared, as did Puckett after a trial on charges of felony false imprisonment and gross misdemeanor sexual conduct. He was acquitted by a jury, but the court of public opinion wasn't so generous.

Although once a courtside fixture at Timberwolves games, Puckett stopped showing his face in public. He moved to Arizona, got engaged, and had plans to marry again.

He used to tell people he wouldn't live past 50. His parents hadn't, so he didn't believe he would, either.

Sadly, he was right.

Puckett died March 7, 2006, a day after suffering a stroke. He was 45.

He was a great player. He wasn't always a great guy.

DOES TONY OLIVA BELONG IN THE HALL OF FAME?

Now that's a stupid question, right? Of course Tony Oliva belongs in the Baseball Hall of Fame.

The Twins outfielder/DH would be in

there, too, if it wasn't for all the self-important writers who do the voting. Inclusion in the Baseball Hall of Fame in Cooperstown, New York, is initially decided by several hundred members of the Baseball Writers' Association of America. Some of them have supported Oliva, but not enough of them. Seventy-five percent of those casting ballots need to endorse a Hall of Fame candidate for him to get in. In the 15 years he was on the writers' ballot (1982–1996), Oliva's highest percentage of votes was 47.31, in 1988.

The writers skipped over Oliva so many times, his Hall of Fame fate has been passed on to the Veterans Committee, which includes living Hall of Fame members, Ford C. Frick recipients, and J.G. Taylor Spink Award winners. The Veterans Committee doesn't vote every year, though, so Oliva's window to get in keeps shrinking. And, of course, he has competition from other former players whose Hall of Fame fate also rests with the Veterans Committee.

Oliva's difficulty getting into the Hall of Fame is due, in part, to his not reaching benchmark statistics that many voters want to see in a Hall of Famer, such as 3,000 hits. Oliva had only 1,917 hits, but there are reasons he didn't have more. Besides the writers, Oliva's knees and other body parts betrayed him. He spent 15 seasons with the Twins (1962–76), but could have gone even longer if not for injuries curtailing his career.

Even with the injuries, Oliva did enough when healthy to belong in the Hall of Fame.

He had an impressive .304 lifetime batting average. And though he fell just short of reaching 2,000 hits or 1,000 RBI, Oliva won 3 American League batting titles and was the first player in history to win titles in his first two major-league seasons. He led the American League in hits five times, led it in doubles four times, and led it in runs once. In 11 full seasons, he hit .300 or better half a dozen times. The 1964 AL Rookie of the Year, Oliva made eight All-Star teams and finished runner-up for the AL's MVP award twice. He also won a Gold Glove for his outfield play. He was one of the premier ball players in an era that included Hall of Famers Hank Aaron, Willie Mays, and Lou Brock, and that's reason enough why Oliva should have a Hall of Fame plaque of his own.

A couple of writers named Lawrence Ritter and Donald Honig included Oliva in their 1981 book, The 100 Greatest Baseball Players of All Time. It's too bad there weren't more writers like those two with a Hall of Fame vote.

Oliva, by the way, is in the Cuban Baseball Hall of Fame.

It's not quite the same thing.

WHAT WAS THE WORST DECISION BY A TWINS EXECUTIVE NOT NAMED CALVIN GRIFFITH?

42 You know what the Twins got for David Ortiz?

It's the same thing you would get if you fed coins into a busted jukebox: nothing.

For years, Twins general manager Terry Ryan has been one of the most astute judges of talent in major league baseball. But he sure whiffed on Ortiz.

Ryan let Ortiz get away. Some of it had to with Ortiz's history of injuries. Some of it had to do with fear that Ortiz would kick the Twins' ass in arbitration. So Ryan, who worked for a terminally cheap owner, didn't even attempt to keep Ortiz in Minnesota after the 2002 season.

By the way, that terminally cheap owner was Carl Pohlad, who bought the Twins from another terminally cheap owner, Calvin Griffith. Griffith made some really bad decisions when he owned the Twins, insulting players with comments and contract offers. He never should have let somebody like Rod Carew get away, but that was Griffith's way. Griffith knew baseball talent. He also knew he didn't want to pay a lot to keep it. Anyway, Ryan knew Ortiz had talent. He just didn't realize how much.

Ortiz, suddenly a free agent, signed with the Boston Red Sox. At first, the Red Sox didn't know what they had, either. He didn't come right in as an everyday player.

Soon enough, though, the Red Sox figured out that their lineup was a lot more dangerous with Ortiz in it. He started alternating between first base and designated hitter. After the 2003 All-Star break, the man known as "Big Papi" hit 28 home runs.

He finished that first season in Boston with 31 homers and 101 RBI, and that was just in 128 games.

In 2004, he had 41 home runs with 139 RBI. After that, he had 47 home runs and 148 RBI in 2005. In 2006, he cracked 54 homers and had 137 RBI.

You take Big Papi out of the Boston lineup in 2004 and you might as well take the World Series trophy away from the Red Sox. He had a walk-off home run to beat the New York Yankees in Game 4 of the American League Championship Series and his walk-off single crumpled the Yankees in Game 5. He was named the MVP of that ALCS. In the four-game World Series sweep of the St. Louis Cardinals, Ortiz kicked in with a home run and 4 RBI and batted .308.

Despite hitting .300 with nearly 50 home runs and 150 RBI in 2005, Ortiz got screwed over in the regular-season MVP voting. A couple of sports writers refused to put him anywhere on their MVP ballots because Ortiz primarily was a designated hitter and, in their twisted sense of what's right, a

109

DH wasn't deserving of their vote. Though he should have been the MVP, Ortiz finished second to Alex Rodriguez.

Meanwhile, as Ortiz was spanking all those home runs in Boston, the Twins were in desperate need of a power hitter. It wasn't until 2006, when first baseman Justin Morneau won the AL's MVP award with 34 home runs and 130 RBI, that the Twins ended a nearly two-decade drought of having nobody hit 30 home runs.

Morneau gave the Twins the much-needed power source they lost when Ryan let Ortiz go. Then again, Morneau didn't offer nearly as much pop. Even as MVP, he still had 20 fewer home runs than Ortiz in 2006.

Imagine if the Twins had Morneau and Ortiz in their lineup. Sadly, that's all Twins fan can do—imagine it.

BESIDES MOLSON BEER, WHAT WAS CANADA'S BEST EXPORT TO MINNESOTA?

43 There's nothing like a cold Molson on just about any day of the year. As Homer Simpson would say, "Mmmm . . . Beer."

Homer's beer of choice is Duff Beer, but that's probably because he never kicked back with a bottle of Molson.

Molson beer is some of the best stuff to come out of Canada and land in Minnesota. Also up near the top of the list of Canadian exports are Wild general manager Doug Risebrough, Wild coach Jacques Lemaire, and Wild assistant coach Mario Tremblay.

Those three were teammates on the Montreal Canadiens' Stanley Cup teams in the 1970s. Those three also have done a fine job with the Wild, building the franchise from scratch and making it one of the most popular teams in the NHL. Although the Wild still were looking for their first Stanley Cup during the 2006–07 season, Lemaire led the New Jersey Devils to the Stanley Cup in 1995 and is one of the best head coaches in the game. And you couldn't do much better for an assistant coach than Tremblay. Plus, Risebrough knows how to construct a team, although he has spent most of his tenure as general manager waiting for ownership to come across with the kind of money necessary to put together a championship bunch.

Oh, yeah, Risebrough, Lemaire, and Tremblay are good. They're just not Canada's best export to Minnesota.

Canada's best export to Minnesota was a baseball player. And, no, it wasn't Corey Koskie, although he is a Canada lad and was a decent third baseman with the Twins when he wasn't on the disabled list.

No, at the top of the list of transplanted Canadians is Justin Morneau.

Admittedly, that is based mostly on just one season with the Twins, but what a season.

In 2006, Morneau won the American League MVP award after batting .321 with 34 home runs and 130 RBI. He became the power hitter the Twins had so desperately needed for nearly two decades. (As mentioned elsewhere, the franchise went from 1987 until 2006 without having somebody hit 30 home runs.)

Born May 21, 1981, in New Westminster, British Columbia, Morneau was a hockey goalie and baseball player as a kid. You can bet the Twins and their fans are happy he chose baseball over hockey, and that the team's scouting department chose him in the third round of the 1999 amateur draft.

Morneau showed glimpses of his power in 2004, when he spent 74 games with the Twins and hit 19 home runs with 54

RBI. That offseason started a run of trouble for him, though. In a rough few months, he had to deal with appendicitis, chicken pox, and a bout with pneumonia that came on the heels of a lung infection. Then, as the 2005 season ramped up, he missed three weeks after getting hit in the helmet with a pitch on April 7. He suffered a concussion and had headaches and dizziness. When you're dealing with concussions, you never know if there will be problems that linger.

Morneau recovered well enough from the head trauma but, in June of that season, he was diagnosed with a bone spur in his left elbow. He kept playing anyway. Things had to get better, right? By the end of the season he had only mustered a .239 batting average, but he still had 22 homers and 79 RBI in 141 games.

Morneau had a slow start in 2006. He was hitting just .236 with 11 home runs and 38 RBI on June 7, the day manager Ron Gardenhire called him into his office to have a talk about staying focused. Morneau found his focus and his batting stroke, and helped lift the Twins to a division title.

New York Yankees shortstop Derek Jeter, who finished second to Morneau in the MVP voting in 2006, issued a statement that called the Twins' first baseman "a special player" and added that he suspected "this won't be the last time you will hear his name mentioned when awards are being passed out."

Jeter isn't the only one to suspect that, which is why, besides Molson beer, Morneau is Canada's best export to Minnesota.

WHICH MINNESOTA ATHLETE GOT THE BEST SEND-OFF TO THE HEREAFTER?

 When athletes or ex-athletes die, fans react. Sometimes, it's with just a quick comment, an "Oh, that's too bad." Other times, it's more than that.

Hundreds of friends, teammates, and fans walked past Korey Stringer's open casket to pay their respects after the Vikings' offensive tackle collapsed during a wickedly hot day at training camp and died hours later at a Mankato hospital.

People were saddened by Stringer's death because it was so sudden and because he still was an athlete in his prime.

But no athlete or ex-athlete ever received the kind of send-off Kirby Puckett did when he died. And chances are, none ever will.

His life suddenly over at the age of 45, just a day after suffering a stroke in March 2006, Puckett did in death what he did when he played outfield for the Minnesota Twins. He touched people.

Almost within moments of his death, people began showing up on the west side of the Metrodome. That's where you'll find 34 Kirby Puckett Place, the main entrance to the Twins' offices and the field where Puckett once reigned. Leaning against a railing just outside that entrance sprang up a tribute like you've never seen. The Twins had nothing to do with it. It was all done by fans.

There were photos of Puckett, as well as Hallmark cards, handmade cards, T-shirts, posters, and Wheaties boxes that commemorated the 1987 World Series. There also were red roses and lighted candles, and even a Puckett bobblehead. There were baseballs with messages scrawled on them. One message, handwritten on a slat of cardboard, had the date Puckett died and this: "The Puck stopped here." Another note, handwritten as well, said it best of all: "There is crying in baseball."

Fans didn't care about the ugly personal stuff that came out about Puckett after his playing days ended. They only cared to remember the good times.

Less than a week after Puckett died, the Twins had a tribute inside the Metrodome. Thousands showed up to say good-bye. There were speeches by friends and ex-teammates. The memories flowed, and so did a few tears.

Maybe some day some Minnesota athlete will have a tribute that rivals Puckett's. But nothing will top it.

WHAT WAS THE BEST SPORTS-RELATED PROMOTION IN MINNESOTA HISTORY?

The best Minnesota sports promotion was just a piece of cloth the size of a handkerchief with some printing on it. But no promotion before and no promotion since has been more popular with Minnesotans than the Homer Hanky.

Oh, a lot of Minnesotans, like many folks around the country, like collecting team-related bobblehead dolls. But no bobblehead has come close to catching on the way the Homer Hanky did.

During the 1987 postseason, particularly the World Series, the Homer Hanky was the must-have item of every Twins fan. If you were old enough to attend a game at the Metrodome or even if you just watched on TV, then you remember all those hankies being waved and shaken like maracas whenever the Twins did something good.

The idea of the Homer Hanky didn't spring from the mind of somebody in the Twins marketing department, however. The Homer Hanky actually was a newspaper promotion. Terry Blair, who worked for the *Minneapolis Star Tribune*, thought putting the Twins' logo in red on a piece of cloth would be a good way to promote the newspaper's coverage of the playoffs. The Homer Hanky, initially handed out at games and then available for a buck at some stores, caught on everywhere in Minnesota . . . except one place. The *St. Paul Pioneer Press* avoided acknowledging its existence, which was a tough thing to do with 60,000 fans waving and shaking the hankies at games. But it was created by a rival newspaper so, as far as *Pioneer Press* writers were concerned, the Homer Hanky didn't exist.

But it did. And it continues to exist and makes a comeback whenever the Twins reach the postseason.

WHO'S THE BEST BASEBALL PLAYER TO COME OUT OF ST. PAUL?

46 Some day, the answer to that question could be Joe Mauer. Not yet, though. Not when you consider the others who were born and raised and learned to play baseball in St. Paul.

Jack Morris is a St. Paul kid, and this 254-game winner and owner of World Series championship rings from three different teams would be the quick and easy answer if the question was, "Who is the best pitcher ever to come out of St. Paul?"

But what we're looking for here is the best everyday ball player with St. Paul on his birth certificate.

It's Paul Molitor.

Or . . .

It's Dave Winfield.

A case could be made for either of them being St. Paul's finest ball player.

Both Molitor and Winfield had long, distinguished careers with several major league teams, including the Twins. They were contemporaries of each other, starting their careers in the 1970s and playing into the 1990s. Both had more than 3,000 hits. Both are in the Hall of Fame.

So, which way should we tilt?

Toward Molitor, who had 3,319 career hits and a career batting average of .306?

Or . . .

Toward Winfield, who had 3,110 career hits and a career batting average of .283?

Besides having more hits and a better batting average, Molitor also had 504 stolen bases compared to Winfield's 223 steals.

Molitor also led the American League in hits three times, something Winfield never did in either league.

And Molitor accumulated his statistics in one less season; he played 21 seasons, whereas Winfield played 22.

With more hits, a better average, and more steals, there are three significant categories where Molitor has the edge.

Molitor could get on base and do damage once he got there.

The thing is, he couldn't clear the bases the way Winfield could.

Winfield had power, a lot more than Molitor. Winfield hit 20 or more home runs 15 times, and 30 or more three times. Molitor only hit more than 20 home runs once, in 1993, when he had 22 homers and 111 RBI.

Only twice in his career did Molitor have more than 100 RBI. Winfield had eight 100-plus RBI seasons.

Winfield had 465 career home runs and 1,833 RBI. Molitor? He had 234 and 1,307, respectively.

Winfield also was a 12-time All-Star and won 7 Gold Gloves for his outfield play. Molitor was a seven-time All-Star. As for Gold Gloves, Molitor won, well, uh, none. Of course, he was shuttled around throughout his career, playing every position except catcher. And, in his last eight seasons, he primarily was a designated hitter.

Before telling you who St. Paul's best ball player is, let's take a moment to give props to the Capital City for producing such fine baseball talent. It's not just coincidence that St. Paul has produced two Hall of Famers, and two others who could some day make it to the Hall of Fame (Morris and Mauer). While there could be something in the water—no tests have been done to find out—St. Paul's reputation for producing exceptional baseball players was built on some terrific youth leagues and the coaches who ran them. (And, of course, genetics played a part. Mauer, Morris, Molitor, and Winfield all come from athletically gifted families.) Minneapolis, however, hasn't been as lucky as St. Paul when it comes to producing genetically exceptional baseball players or having the same kind of outstanding youth baseball programs.

OK, back to the argument.

Like we said earlier, both Molitor and Winfield had long, distinguished careers. But what distinguished Winfield even more was his power, and that's also what makes him the best ball player to come out of St. Paul.

WHO WAS MINNESOTA'S FIRST GREAT HOME RUN HITTER?

 Nope, it wasn't Harmon Killebrew. Harmon is Minnesota's all-time greatest home run hitter, but he wasn't the first guy in the state to knock a lot of balls over a fence.

Long before Killebrew's arrival in Minnesota in 1961, there was a ball player named Percival Wherritt Werden, "Moose" to those who knew him.

Born in St. Louis in 1865, "Moose" played his ball back in the 19th century, starting out as a pitcher. In 1884, he went 12–1 with a 1.97 ERA for the St. Louis Maroons of the Union

Association, one of the professional leagues back then.

An injury to his arm put the kibosh on Werden's pitching career, so he moved to first base. When Werden was with Toledo in the American Association in 1890 and with the National League's St. Louis Cardinals in 1893, he led those leagues in triples. In fact, Ol'Moose had himself a nice statistical season in 1893. He had just one home run, but he had 94 RBI, 11 stolen bases, a .276 batting average, and those league-leading 29 triples. So, he did what any ball player coming off a fine season might do. He asked for a raise.

And that's how he wound up in Minnesota.

The Cardinals' ownership, in no mood to dicker with a ball player over salary, sold Moose to the Minneapolis Millers of the Western League.

He flourished in the Millers' dimensionally challenged Athletic Park. In 1894, his first year with the Millers and their tiny ballpark, Moose hit 42 home runs and batted .417.

In 1895, he did even better, cracking 45 homers with a .428 average. While the tiny ballpark played a part, nobody else with the Millers came close to hitting as many home runs as Werden did. So, this power surge wasn't just because he played in a bandbox.

No professional ball player would have more home runs than those 45 until 1920, when a fellow named Babe Ruth hit 54 in his first season with the New York Yankees. Before that, Moose Werden was the only pro baseball player with more than 29 home runs.

Moose returned to the National League in 1897, joining the Louisville Colonels. He had a decent year for a lousy 52–78 team, hitting .302 with 5 home runs and 83 RBI.

Moose Werden never again put up huge power numbers. Then again, so what? That doesn't change the simple fact that he was Minnesota's first great home run hitter.

WHO IS MINNESOTA'S MOST FORGOTTEN HALL OF FAMER?

 Well, it's certainly not Harmon Killebrew or Kirby Puckett.

Or Rod Carew.

Or Dave Winfield.

Or Paul Molitor.

It's not Steve Carlton, either.

All six of the Hall of Famers just mentioned put in time with the Twins, some more than others. Killebrew and Puckett, of course, are remembered for what they did as Twins. Carew, meanwhile, spent twelve of his nineteen seasons in Minnesota. Molitor played the final three seasons of his 21-year career with the Twins, while Winfield and Carlton each spent two seasons in Minnesota at the end of their playing days.

The man we're talking about never played for the Twins. He couldn't. The Twins didn't exist when he did his work.

This Hall of Famer made his major league debut in 1903. His name was Charles Albert Bender, often called Chief Bender. Nowadays, it would be a politically incorrect nickname because of Bender's Native American heritage. His mother was Ojibwe, and his father was a German settler who found his way to Minnesota.

Bender was born in Brainerd on May 5, 1884. He was a pitcher, one of the best.

On the Baseball Hall of Fame's official website, there's a quote about Bender by Connie Mack, Bender's manager with the Philadelphia Athletics when he played for them from 1903–14. Ol'Connie said of Bender, "If I had all the men I ever handled and they were in their prime and there was one game I wanted to win above all others, Albert would be my man."

Bender won 212 games and had a 2.46 ERA in a 16-year career that included five World Series, all with the A's. He had a 6–4 record and a 2.44 ERA average in ten World Series games. In the 1911 World Series, he pitched three complete games in a six-game series won by the Athletics. Bender had a 2–1 record in that series, including a victory in the final game.

Credited with inventing the slider, Bender led the American League in winning percentage three times and possessed, as the Hall of Fame's website put it, "a solid fastball, excellent curveball and outstanding control."

Apparently, he also had excellent emotional control. When people called him "Chief," he was known to tip his cap. When taunted because of his heritage, he sometimes shouted back,

"Foreigners!" When it came to signing autographs, it wasn't as Chief Bender. He signed his name, "Charley Bender."

Bender didn't spend much of his life in Minnesota. He moved to Philadelphia to attend a church-run school when he was eight. At thirteen, he attended the Carlisle Indian Industrial School in Carlisle, Pennsylvania, which produced other famous athletes, such as Jim Thorpe.

Though Philadelphia and other parts of Pennsylvania were where he spent most of his days, which ended at the age of seventy in Philly, Charles Albert Bender is linked to Minnesota because it's where he was born.

It's also where he holds the distinction of being the Minnesota Hall of Famer that we've forgotten most.

WHO MADE THE GREATEST CATCH IN MINNESOTA HISTORY?

49 Actor Sam Shepard began dating Academy Award-winning actress Jessica Lange in 1982. A striking blonde who was born in the northeast Minnesota city of Cloquet, Lange was a great catch for Shepard.

But this isn't about that kind of catch. It's about catching a ball.

Randy Moss was the most explosive wide receiver the Vikings ever had. And, when he wanted to be, he was the most dangerous deep threat in NFL history. Moss made some spectacular catches. He just didn't make the greatest catch in Minnesota history.

No wide receiver could make the sideline catch the way Cris Carter could. Two hands, one hand, a couple of finger-tips; whatever it took, Carter would haul that ball in when he played for the Vikings. Like Moss, Carter made a lot of great catches . . . just not the greatest.

Back in the 1980s, Anthony Carter of the Vikings was either the best wide receiver in the league, or the second best after San Francisco's Jerry Rice, depending on who was doing the rankings. Carter could move the chains and impact the outcome of games with his catches.

It wasn't him, either.

It wasn't even a football player who made that greatest catch in Minnesota history, and you already know it wasn't an actor.

It was a baseball player: Kirby Puckett, in Game 6 of the 1991 World Series.

By reaching over the plexiglass wall at the Metrodome, Puck hijacked a 3rd-inning home run from Ron Gant of the Atlanta Braves, which, in turn, robbed the Braves of a chance to break open the game.

Puck's catch kept the game tight.

Puck's catch forced the game into extra innings.

Puck's catch allowed Puck to win the game with a home run in the 11th inning.

Puck's catch forced a Game 7 and put the Twins in position to win their second World Series in five seasons.

And that's why Puck's catch was the greatest catch in Minnesota history.

WHO WAS A BETTER GOLD GLOVE CENTER FIELDER, KIRBY OR TORII?

50 If you've been reading this book chronologically you know where we stand on Kirby Puckett's leaping catch that robbed Ron Gant and the Atlanta Braves of a home run in Game 6 of the 1991 World Series. It was to Minnesotans what Dwight Clark's leaping end zone grab was to San Francisco 49ers fans in the 1982 NFL playoffs: "the catch."

And while other snags didn't have the historical impact of that grab, Puckett made a number of spectacular catches during his 12-year Hall of Fame career with the Twins. Puckett, of course, didn't just make the dazzling kind of catches that show up on ESPN *SportsCenter* during the baseball season. He made the routine catch as well as the tough catch, and he made them all look so easy. You don't win 6 Gold Gloves, as Puckett did, without catching just about everything hit in the same zip code.

In those dozen seasons with the Twins, most of them spent patrolling center field, Puckett had a .989 fielding percentage. In other words, in 1,696 games in the outfield, he had nearly 4,500 chances to catch the ball and he committed just 51 errors.

Torii Hunter did even better than that through eight seasons with the Twins. After the 2006 season, Hunter had a .991 fielding percentage. In 1,048 games as an outfielder, Hunter had nearly 2,700 opportunities to catch the ball and had just 26 errors.

Two of Hunter's errors stick out above the others because they came in different postseasons against the Oakland A's. In Game 3 of the 2002 American League division playoffs, Hunter tried to make a shoestring catch of a ball hit by Ray Durham. The ball scooted under his glove and reached the wall for an inside-the-park home run. In Game 2 of the 2006 divisional series, the scored tied 2–2 and a runner on first, Hunter dove for a ball hit by Mark Kotsay. The safe play would have been to keep the ball in front of him and let Kotsay come away with a single. That's not Hunter's style, though. He's confident in his ability to get to balls. And Hunter might have gotten to Kotsay's if it hadn't tailed away from him as he dove. That ball, like Durham's, became an inside-the-park home run.

Afterward, Hunter let reporters in on just how disappointed he was, telling them, "I feel less than a man right now."

He also made sure to mention he still felt he was the best center fielder in the game.

And he was right. Those two misplays had bad outcomes, but they didn't alter the fact that Hunter was baseball's best defensive center fielder, and still the best Gold Glove center fielder in Twins history.

Yep, even above Puckett.

Like Puckett, Hunter won 6 Gold Gloves, and that was in four fewer seasons and just through the 2006 season. There could be more. Hunter even won a Gold Glove in 2005 despite missing 64 games with a fractured left ankle. That injury even speaks to his prowess—it came when Hunter tried climbing the wall at Fenway Park to steal a home run, and his spikes caught in the fence padding.

With a bat, it's no contest. Puckett crushes Hunter. But with a glove, well, it's a different story. Hunter is faster than Puckett, and he could leap higher than Puckett. Because of his speed and leaping ability, he has been able to make catches that Puckett wouldn't have attempted, or been in position to attempt.

That's not a knock on Puckett. He was an incredibly gifted fielder. But if he and Hunter had been on the same team, Puckett likely would have made the shift to right field, as he did for the final couple of seasons of his career. By then, the 1994 and 1995 seasons, Puckett was finished winning Gold Gloves and he was entering his mid-30s, and the Twins wanted younger, fresher legs in center field. Nobody caught on in center, though, until Hunter arrived. He played in one game in 1997, six games in 1998, and stuck around for good starting in 1999.

Actually, it wasn't for good.

It was for greatness as a Gold Glove center fielder.

WHO WAS THE BEST HALL OF FAME CENTER FIELDER EVER TO PLAY FOR A MINNESOTA TEAM?

51

It wasn't Kirby Puckett.

Okay, we admit it. This is a trick question. The best center fielder ever to play for a Minnesota team didn't play for the Twins.

He played in the minor leagues for the Minneapolis Millers way back in 1951, when the Millers were members of the American Association.

His name was Willie Mays.

Also known as "The Say Hey Kid," Mays didn't last long with the Millers; just 35 games. But during that stretch, Mays played center field and hit .477 with eight home runs and 30 RBI. And the reason his Millers career was so brief was that the New York Giants called him up to the majors, where he played for 22 seasons in a Hall of Fame career that included 660 home runs, 1,903 RBI, 3,283 hits, a .302 batting average, and 12 Gold Gloves.

You remember how Puckett's leaping catch stole a home

run from Ron Gant in Game 6 of the 1991 World Series? That was pretty special, right? Well, in the 1954 World Series, Mays' over-the-shoulder catch of Vic Wertz's deep fly ball remains one of the greatest moments in baseball history. It was said that Mays' glove was "where triples go to die."

Mays had a simple explanation for the way he played: "They throw the ball, I hit it. They hit the ball, I catch it."

Los Angeles Dodgers pitcher Sandy Koufax once said, "I can't believe that Babe Ruth was a better player than Willie Mays. Ruth is to baseball what Arnold Palmer is to golf. He got the game moving. But I can't believe he could run as well as Mays, and I can't believe he was any better an outfielder."

You'd get no argument from Mays, who said, "I think I was the best baseball player I ever saw."

Willie Mays was the best center fielder ever to play for a Minnesota baseball team, that's for sure.

WHICH TWINS WOULD YOU WANT IN CRUNCH TIME?

52

Here are the Twins you would want at the plate or on the mound when . . .

THERE ARE TWO OUTS IN THE BOTTOM OF THE NINTH AND YOU'RE DOWN BY THREE RUNS.

This one sounds easy. You can end the game with a grand slam, so you just go with Harmon Killebrew, right? He did have 573 career home runs and his nickname was "Killer." And he is the Twins' all-time leader in grand slams, with 10 in 14 seasons in Minnesota. He'd make a good choice . . . a good second choice. Killer might get you that grand slam, or he might strike out. He had almost three times as many strike-outs (1,699) as he did home runs in his career.

So we're going with Kirby Puckett. When Puck played, there was no better clutch performer in the game. Though he had only 207 career home runs, he smacked 7 grand slams over 12 seasons with the Twins. And with his .318 career batting average, which is 62 points higher than Killebrew's career average, the odds were Puck would at least get a hit and knock in a few of the runs to make it easier for the next guy up, who likely would be Kent Hrbek. Herbie had 8 career home runs in 14 seasons with the Twins. He also had 293 career home runs and a .282 batting average.

YOU NEED A PINCH HITTER TO KEEP ALIVE A RALLY, OR GET ONE GOING.

You'd want Puckett, but he already would be in the game. You could go with Randy Bush, who led the Twins in pinch hits in five different seasons. You go with Bush. We're going with Gene Larkin, who had the biggest pinch hit in the history of the franchise. The Twins won the 1991 World Series in the bottom of the 10th inning when his single over a drawn-in outfield scored Dan Gladden from third.

YOU WANT TO STOMP THE OTHER TEAM'S MOMENTUM WITH A LEADOFF HOME RUN.

Chuck Knoblauch had 14 leadoff home runs in seven seasons with the Twins. That's second-most in team history and 6 leadoff homers behind the leader: Jacque Jones. His 20 home runs from 1999–2005 make Jones the pick here.

YOU NEED A STOLEN BASE.

The Twins never have had a ridiculously scary base stealer, but Knoblauch is the all-time leader with 276 stolen bases and is as good a choice as any.

YOU NEED SOMEONE TO PITCH A BIG GAME.

This is a no-brainer. You go with Jack Morris, one of the biggest big-game performers in history. See his ten-inning masterpiece in Game 7 of the 1991 World Series for details.

YOU NEED A PITCHER TO BE THE STAFF ACE FOR AN ENTIRE SEASON.

The Twins have had some impressive pitchers over the years, including Morris, Jim Kaat, Jim Perry, Mudcat Grant, Bert Blyleven, and Brad Radke. But none were ever better than Johan Santana, who won his second Cy Young Award with the Twins in 2006. Santana, who joined the Twins in 2000 and didn't pitch more than 160 innings until 2004, won his first Cy Young Award in 2004, when he went 20–6 with a 2.61 ERA that led the American League. In 2006, he went 19–6 with a 2.77 ERA that once again led the American League. In 2005, Santana finished third in the Cy Young voting with a 16–7 record and a 2.87 ERA, the AL's second best.

YOU NEED A CLOSER.

You've got some good choices, such as Jeff Reardon, who handled closing chores for the 1987 World Series team, and Rick Aguilera, who closed for the 1991 team. There's also Eddie Guardado and Joe Nathan. The nod goes to Aguilera, whose 254 saves between 1989 and 1999 are the most in team history. He also had 2 saves and a win in the 1991 World Series. Aguilera could be overtaken at some point by Nathan, who had 124 saves in his first three seasons with the Twins (2004–06).

WHO SHOULD PUCKETT AND MORRIS HAVE THANKED FOR THEIR 1991 WORLD SERIES RINGS?

53

Well, they could have started off by thanking each other. Morris doesn't get to pitch his Game 7 gem if Puckett doesn't win Game 6 with a home run.

But the ball player both Morris and Puckett should have given the biggest pat on the back to, other than each other, was Gene Larkin.

Morris was the winning pitcher in Game 7, throwing 10 innings of no-run ball, but it was Larkin who won the game with his pinch-hit single in the bottom of the 10th.

The inning began with a double by Dan Gladden, who was sacrificed to third by Chuck Knoblauch.

Rather than risk having one of the Twins' two most dangerous hitters end the game, Atlanta Braves manager Bobby Cox called for intentional walks to Kirby Puckett and Kent Hrbek. That loaded the bases for Larkin.

When the inning began, Larkin went over in his mind who he might be called upon to replace as a pinch hitter. He did a mental scan of the batting order: Gladden, Knoblauch, Puckett, Hrbek, then Jarvis Brown.

Jarvis Brown?

Larkin knew if the Twins still were alive in the inning, he'd be hitting for Brown, who had been sent in an inning earlier as a pinch runner for Chili Davis.

Larkin was right.

He went to the plate to face Braves reliever Alejandro Pena, who served up a fastball, out and over the plate.

Whack.

With Atlanta's outfield drawn in, Larkin singled over left fielder Brian Hunter to win the game 1–0 and the Series 4–3.

A decade later, in 2001, people still remembered what Puckett did in Game 6 and what Morris did in Game 7, as well as what Larkin did.

"People want to thank me, congratulate me or tell me how happy that hit makes them feel," Larkin said in July 2001. "It was one of the bigger moments in my life. I was a role player, an average player, at best. If I didn't get this hit, I'd be just another player who had a so-so career."

Instead, he took a swing into history.

"I can tell you how I felt going to the batter's box. I was very nervous," Larkin said. "My knees were kind of shaking. I remember saying to myself, 'Hit the first strike.' I didn't want the umpire to dictate whether it was a strike or not. I wanted to hit the first strike and get out of there. I never felt I wasn't going to do the job. I felt I would get a sacrifice fly or a hit. I was supremely confident. It was a win-win situation because I was a contact hitter."

It was a win-win: Win the game, win the World Series.

Kirby Puckett, Jack Morris, and a lot of other Twins and their fans had Larkin to thank for that.

WHO WOULD BE IN THE TWINS' ALL-TIME BEST BATTING ORDER?

 One rule: We only count statistics from seasons a player had with the Twins. So, you could be a Hall of Famer, as Dave Winfield is, and not make the cut.

That said, here is the Twins' all-time kick-ass batting order, with a quick blurb on each player:

ROD CAREW, 2B

This Hall of Famer won 7 AL batting titles in twelve seasons with the Twins (1967–78), had 3,053 career hits, and held a career batting average of .328.

TONY OLIVA, RF

Oliva led the American League in hits five times, won three league batting titles, and had a .304 career batting average.

KIRBY PUCKETT, CF

This Hall of Famer was the ignition switch for the Twins' two World Series championships.

HARMON KILLEBREW, 3B

This Hall of Famer with 573 career home runs played only 178 fewer games at third than he did at first.

KENT HRBEK, 1B

The team's best defensive first baseman had 25 or more home runs six times, and 20 or more homers 10 times, in 14 seasons (1981–94).

JOE MAUER, C

No apologies to Earl Battey; Mauer won the 2006 AL batting title with a .347 average, and that's what puts him here.

PAUL MOLITOR, DH

This Hall of Famer with 3,319 career hits had 113 RBI, a .341 average, and 18 stolen bases in his first of three seasons with the Twins (1996–98) at the end of his career.

BOB ALLISON, LF

Allison never hit better than .287 in a season, but averaged 31 home runs and 96 RBI in the Twins' first four seasons in Minnesota, so he adds some pop at the bottom of this lineup.

ZOILO VERSALLES, SS

Versalles had five .300-plus seasons with the Twins (1961–67), four seasons with double-digit home runs, and four with double-digit steals.

WHO'S ON THE TWINS' ALL-TIME PITCHING STAFF?

 We're going with five starters and five relievers. And with the relievers we're picking, you never would have to worry about being without a closer.

Beginning with the ace of the staff, here is the starting rotation:

1. JOHAN SANTANA (LEFTY)

Santana had two Cy Young Awards before the age of 28.

2. JACK MORRIS (RIGHTY)

Morris, the best big-game pitcher on the staff, went 10 innings to win Game 7 of the 1991 World Series.

3. BERT BLYLEVEN (RIGHTY)

Blyleven had 287 career wins, a 3.31 career ERA, and is

fifth all-time in the majors with 2,035 strikeouts.

4. FRANK VIOLA (LEFTY)

Viola won the AL Cy Young Award for the Twins in 1988 when he went 24–7 with a 2.64 ERA.

5. JIM KAAT (LEFTY)

Kaat won 283 games with a 3.45 career ERA, including a 1966 season with the Twins when he went 25–13 with a 2.75 ERA.

And now, the top relievers:

1. RICK AGUILERA (RIGHTY)

Aguilera had 30 or more saves in his first four seasons with the Twins, and had ERAs ranging from 2.35 to 3.11 over that span; he saved 42 games for the 1991 World Series championship team.

2. JOE NATHAN (RIGHTY)

Nathan had 44, 43, and 36 saves in his first three seasons with the Twins (2004–06) and had ERAs of 1.62, 2.70, and 1.58.

3. JEFF REARDON (RIGHTY)

Reardon spent only three seasons with the Twins (1987–89), but made them memorable ones with 31, 42, and 31 saves.

4. EDDIE GUARDADO (LEFTY)

Guardado began his career as a set-up man, then became a top closer with 45 and 41 saves in 2002 and 2003.

5. LATROY HAWKINS (RIGHTY)

Much better as a set-up man than a closer, Hawkins went 9–3 with a 1.86 ERA as a reliever in 2003.

WHICH TWINS HAD THE BEST NICKNAMES?

56

You'll find athletes in every sport with nicknames. But no sport is like baseball.

In baseball, you will find wonderful and colorful nicknames, such as Shoeless Joe (Jackson), Oil Can (Boyd), Stan the Man (Musial), The Splendid Splinter (Ted Williams), The Big Unit (Randy Johnson), Big Train (Walter Johnson), and the Sultan of Swat, a.k.a., The Babe (Ruth).

Members of the Twins were given some fun and interesting nicknames before, during, and after playing with the team. Here, in ascending order, are the ten best nicknames of Twins players.

10. PUCK

Sure, it's just a shortened version of his last name, but whenever anyone says Puck, you instantly know they are talking about the Twins' most popular player ever, Kirby Puckett.

9. THE TERMINATOR

As a closer, it was Jeff Reardon's job to terminate the opposition; hence, the nickname.

8. EVERYDAY EDDIE

This name was given to reliever Eddie Guardado because, well, you could send him to the mound every day.

7. KITTY

It should be self-explanatory how Jim Kaat got the nickname, but if you're having trouble figuring it out, think kitty cat. Get it? Kitty Kaat.

6. KILLER

Harmon Killebrew's bat could kill an opposing team, and when your last name begins with the letters Kille, it's only natural for you to be called that.

5. EL GUAPO

Only a member of the Twins for two seasons (1990 and 1993), pitcher Rich Garces reportedly was pinned with the nickname by a teammate who claimed he looked like the bad guy in the Steve Martin movie *The Three Amigos*.

4. CHILI

The way the story goes, Charles Theodore Davis was just 12 years old when a lousy haircut made it look as if he got a trim with a bowl on his head. So, he was tagged with the nickname "Chili Bowl," eventually whittled to Chili. It was how everyone came to know Chili Davis, the Twins' designated hitter in 1991 and 1992.

3. BIG PAPI

Spanish for daddy, David Ortiz has indeed been the big daddy of home runs in the American League over the past few seasons. It's too bad for the Twins that Ortiz didn't get the chance to show the extent of his Big Papi power while playing a limited role with them (1997–2002). The nickname really caught on in Boston.

2. SWEET MUSIC

A viola is a musical instrument, and when Frank Viola pitched the hope was that he would make sweet music on the mound. Often, he did.

1. MUDCAT

Just as George Herman Ruth wasn't called by his given name, nobody called Jim Grant by his given name when he pitched in the major leagues. He was Mudcat Grant. The first African American pitcher in the minor leagues to win twenty games, Mudcat went 21–7 with six shutouts and a 3.30 ERA in helping

143

the Twins reach the 1965 World Series. He became the first African American in the American League to win a World Series game. He won Games 1 and 6. Grant got the Mudcat nickname while a minor leaguer with the Cleveland Indians in the 1950s. It was at a time when African American ball players still were being integrated into the major leagues. "Most black players, they thought they were from Mississippi," Grant told *The Lompoc Record*, a California newspaper, in April 2006. "That was just the thing back in those days. Somebody said, 'He's ugly. He looks like a mudcat from Mississippi.'"

WHO WAS THE TRUE VOICE OF THE TWINS?

Ordinarily, when you talk about the voice of a team, you're talking about a long-time radio play-by-play man. For example, Vin Scully, the voice of the Los Angeles Dodgers; Harry Caray, the voice of the Chicago Cubs; and Mel Allen, the voice of the New York Yankees.

Herb Carneal became the radio voice of the Twins in 1962. But he wasn't the true voice of the Twins.

No, the voice of the Twins from their first game in Minnesota until his death in March 2005 was Bob Casey, the public address announcer. Casey was on the mike for the first pitch at Metropolitan Stadium in 1961 and he still was at it in 2004, despite having liver cancer.

Casey became immensely popular with fans and players. In fact, he was so popular with players that, when he knew his death was near, he asked Jack Morris, Kent Hrbek, Tony Oliva, Dan Gladden, Harmon Killebrew, and Kirby Puckett to be his pallbearers. All said yes, though Twins President Dave St. Peter and Twins broadcaster John Gordon wound up filling in for Killebrew and Puckett.

Casey had two signature lines. His introduction of Kirby Puckett became a crowd favorite: "Kir-BEEEEEEE PUCK-it!" And so did the way he would bark out, "There is no smoking in the Metrodome. NO SMOKING!" After Casey's death at 79, the Twins continued playing a tape of him saying "NO SMOK-ING!" at home games.

While he had no trouble with Puckett's name, Casey did struggle with a few others. That was part of his charm.

"He'd butcher anybody's name," Kent Hrbek said. "When I first came up with the Twins, he introduced me as 'Kint.' People thought I spelled it K-I-N-T."

Casey was a source of amusement for players, and not just for the way he pronounced their names.

"There was the time Gorman Thomas popped up," Hrbek said, recounting the incident involving the former Milwaukee Brewers slugger. "Any time Gorman struck out or popped out, he would fling his bat. Well, he flung it behind him at the cage Casey sat in behind home plate. It hit the plastic in front

145

of Casey, and Casey went over backwards. I just cracked up."

And then there was the bomb scare at the old Met in the mid-1970s. "I was just a kid then. I lived near the Met and was there for the game," said Hrbek, who could see the stadium lights from his Bloomington home. "The Twins told Bob to let everyone know to leave the stadium without getting them to panic. So, he yells into the microphone, 'Ladies and gentlemen, we've just been notified there's a BOMB SCARE!'"

The real scare would come decades later, when the true voice of the Twins was gone. There was a giant void. The Twins and their fans knew they would find another public address announcer, but everyone knew they'd never find another Bob Casey.

WHO WILL THE TWINS' ACE BE WHEN THEIR NEW STADIUM OPENS?

58 The quick, easy, and safe answer to that is Johan Santana. He won two of the three Cy Young Awards handed out in the American League between 2004 and 2006. His stuff wasn't just good. It wasn't just nasty. It was good and nasty.

It is likely Santana will be the ace of the Twins' staff when the team's new stadium opens in Minneapolis in 2010.

Then again . . .

By 2010, Santana could be the Twins' second-best pitcher. And it wouldn't be because his skills diminished any. Santana still could be mowing 'em down, racking up wins while keeping his ERA in the cellar.

The reason Santana would drop a notch in the rotation would be Francisco Liriano.

He could be even better than Santana.

Liriano was the better pitcher for part of the 2006 season, a season after which Santana won his second Cy Young Award.

The Twins and their fans will have to wait a while to find out just how good Liriano will be and whether he can overtake Santana as not only the Twins' best pitcher but also the best pitcher in baseball.

After an injury-shortened 2006 season during which he went 12–3 with a 2.16 ERA, Liriano underwent ligament replacement surgery in his left elbow in November 2006. A lefty born in October 1983, he was advised not to play during the 2007 season.

Before his elbow began nagging him in late July 2006, Liriano was the most dominant pitcher in the game. Yeah, even more dominant than Santana.

Santana's 2.77 ERA was the best in the majors in 2006. Liriano's 2.16 ERA would have beaten that if he had pitched enough innings to qualify for the title. Santana had a major-league best 245 strikeouts in 233 2/3 innings. Liriano might have topped that, too. He finished with 144 strikeouts in 121 innings.

With a fastball in the upper 90s and a killer slider, Liriano began the 2006 season in the bullpen. Promoted to the starting rotation in May, he kicked ass. He went 10–1 with a 1.83 ERA in the first half of the season and was named to the All-Star team. Over the season's final two months, with an ache in his elbow, Liriano pitched only six innings in 2 soreness-shortened starts.

Liriano admitted he felt pain during 5 of his starts and never told the team. That pain impacted the way he pitched. In other words, he could have been even more dominant if he had been healthy. He could have won that Cy Young Award instead of Santana. And the Twins could have run off with the AL Central instead of winning it on the final day of the regular season.

If, and it's an extremely huge if, Liriano is able to return in 2008 and dominate batters the way he did when he was healthy, he could leapfrog Santana, and be the Twins' ace when their new stadium opens.

PRO
BASKETBALL

WHO WAS MINNESOTA'S GREATEST PRO ATHLETE?

59 Kirby Puckett, yeah, he was pretty special. Ask anyone who watched him play in the 1987 or 1991 World Series and they'll probably tell you he's Minnesota's most popular athlete ever.

They also may tell you Puckett is Minnesota's greatest pro athlete ever. They'd be wrong. Kevin Garnett? It's not him, either. Harmon Killebrew? Alan Page? Randy Moss?

Nope, nope, and nope.

George Mikan. He's the correct answer.

Many may guess wrong, because most of the people who saw Mikan play basketball either are now a memory or at the tail end of their lives. Mikan did his stuff in the 1940s and 1950s, and because it was so long ago, people don't just tend to forget. They tend to ignore.

But Mikan was the center and the centerpiece of pro basketball's first dynasty. He didn't look like much, if you just looked at his angular face. He wasn't particularly handsome. He wore glasses. Then again, so did Clark Kent.

Mikan was 6-foot-10, and could do things with a basketball

nobody else could in those days.

Puckett and the Twins won two World Series championships. Mikan led the Minneapolis Lakers to five NBA championships in six seasons. Throw in the title the Lakers won in the old National Basketball League, and it was six championships in seven seasons (1947–48 to 1953–54). In 1950, the Associated Press voted Mikan the best basketball player in the first half of the century, and he had only just begun knocking down league championships.

Chances are, the Lakers would have won seven league titles in a row if Mikan hadn't fractured his leg late in the 1950–51 season (a season, by the way, in which he averaged a league-high 28.4 points).

After that season, the NBA widened the width of the foul lane, doubling it from 6 to 12 feet, because of Mikan and the way he dominated inside. It didn't stop him, or even diminish his impact on the game. He adapted and led the Lakers to three more league titles.

In the midst of all those league championships, Mikan won scoring titles and was a dominant rebounder. He averaged 22.6 points and nearly ten rebounds a game in a Hall of Fame career that lasted nine years.

Mikan, of course, didn't win all those NBA championships by himself. There were other Lakers who were fine players, men like Jim Pollard, Slater Martin, Vern Mikkelsen, and Clyde Lovellette. All were exceptional in their own right. But this was Mikan's team, and everyone knew it. When the

Lakers went to play the New York Knicks at Madison Square Garden in December 1949, the marquee at the Garden didn't say, "Lakers vs. Knicks." It said, "Geo. Mikan vs. Knicks."

After the Lakers left Minneapolis, they had some terrific centers: Wilt Chamberlain, Kareem Abdul-Jabbar, and Shaquille O'Neal. None of them did what Mikan did. None of them won as many NBA titles with the Lakers. None of them had the dimensions of the court changed because of him.

Without Mikan, the Minneapolis Lakers would have been just another team. With him, they were dynamic and dynastic.

IF KEVIN GARNETT IS SO GREAT, WHY DIDN'T HE RACK UP NBA TITLES?

60 He never liked being identified as being 7 feet tall, you know. Kevin Garnett always insisted he be listed at 6-foot-11. His old coach with the Timberwolves, Flip Saunders, used to say Garnett was 6-foot-12. In reality, he was more like 6-foot-13.

Height denial isn't the only thing that's odd about Garnett. It's also odd, to some people anyway, that the man once known as Da Kid reached 30 years of age and hadn't even gotten a whiff of the NBA Finals, let alone won a championship.

Others, meanwhile, don't find it so odd. There are folks out there who believe Garnett, while possessed with enormous skill and talent, is more of a Scottie Pippen than a Michael Jordan. In other words, KG needed a superstar to carry him and the Timberwolves to a title.

Garnett didn't do much to debunk that theory with the way he shied away from being the go-to guy in the final seconds of a game. Throughout his career with the Wolves, which ended in the summer of 2007 with a trade to the Boston Celtics, KG always seemed to want somebody else to grab the game by the scruff of the neck and win it. Not like Michael Jordan, who always wanted the ball when the outcome was tezetering.

Magic Johnson, Larry Bird, Kobe Bryant; most great players who led their teams to championships wanted the rock come crunch time.

Early in his career, Garnett and his advisors made a decision that also impacted his chances of winning an NBA title. They decided KG should be filthy rich, richer than anyone else in the NBA.

The Timberwolves went along with this and gave Garnett monster contracts. When he signed for $126 million, Garnett said it wasn't about the loot. Yeah, right.

By the way, did you know it would take somebody with an annual income of $50,000 more than 2,500 years to make $126 million?

Anyway, Garnett's loot made it difficult for the Timberwolves to have much money left over to spend on players who might actually help win a title.

The Timberwolves came closest during the 2003–04 season, when they added Latrell Sprewell and Sam Cassell. That year they reached the Western Conference finals before bombing out against the Los Angeles Lakers. That year marked the first time Garnett ever got out of the first round of the playoffs.

He could score and he could rebound, he often led the NBA in double doubles, and when it came to accumulating statistics or loot, you'd always find Garnett's name among the league leaders.

What you won't find is his name associated with an NBA title.

WHO WAS MINNESOTA'S BEST HOMEGROWN BASKETBALL PLAYER?

61 George Mikan was the best basketball player ever to play for a Minnesota team. He changed how the center position was played back when he was leading the Minneapolis Lakers to NBA titles. But he wasn't from Minnesota. He was born in Joliet, Illinois, and played his college ball at DePaul.

After Mikan, Kevin Garnett goes down as the next-best

basketball player ever to play for a Minnesota team. Whenever he stepped on the court, he often was the best player in the game. He wasn't a Minnesota native, either, though. He was born in Mauldin, South Carolina, and the Timberwolves drafted him out of Farragut Academy, a high school in Chicago.

Rick Rickert was a homegrown Minnesota basketball player. So was Joel Przybilla and Kris Humphries. They all were great high school basketball players who were decent at the next levels.

Lindsay Whalen was better than any of them. After a standout high school career in Hutchinson, Whalen went to the University of Minnesota and became one of the best players in women's college basketball.

Whalen was the 2002 Big Ten Player of the Year, only the third sophomore to win the award in conference history. She made All-America teams her junior and senior seasons, and led the Gophers to the women's Final Four. The Connecticut Sun made her the fourth overall pick of the 2004 WNBA draft, and Whalen quickly became one of that league's best point guards.

She's second on the list of Minnesota's best homegrown basketball players.

First? That would be Kevin McHale.

It's tough to beat what McHale did in his basketball career. In high school, he led Hibbing to the state finals. At the University of Minnesota, he averaged 15.2 points and 8.5

rebounds a game and was named first-team All Big Ten twice. It's what he did in the NBA, though, that sets McHale head and broad shoulders above everyone else.

Playing alongside fellow forward Larry Bird, McHale helped the Boston Celtics win three NBA championships in the 1980s. Over a 13-year career with the Celtics, McHale was one of the best inside players the game has ever known. Former NBA coach Hubie Brown once told the *Boston Globe* that McHale "became the most difficult low-post player to defend, once he made the catch, in the history of the league. He was totally unstoppable because of his quickness, diversification of moves and the long arms that gave him an angle to release the ball over a taller man or more explosive jumper."

McHale also could play some wicked D. He was named to the league's All-Defensive first team three times, and to its second team another three times. He is in the Basketball Hall of Fame and, in 1996, was named one of the 50 Greatest Players in NBA History.

McHale went from playing basketball to running basketball operations for the Timberwolves. Timberwolves fans everywhere wish that, as an executive, McHale could have even a fraction of the success he had as a player.

DID A PSYCHIC FORETELL THE COMING OF KEVIN GARNETT AND STEPHON MARBURY?

62 A lot of people believe in psychics the way they believe in vampires, alien life forms, and benevolent oil company executives. They just don't buy into them.

But maybe those people don't know about the Minnesota psychic who predicted the Timberwolves would wind up with Kevin Garnett and Stephon Marbury—before anyone else, including the Timberwolves, knew.

Okay, technically, the psychic didn't offer up Garnett and Marbury by name. But she came pretty darn close.

In 1993, a few years before the Timberwolves drafted Garnett, Edina-based psychic Ruth Lordan told a *Pioneer Press* columnist that the team wouldn't be any good until it selected a nineteen-year-old high school player in the NBA draft.

A high school kid? At the time, it was an absurd thought. No high school player had been drafted by an NBA team in decades. Well, Garnett came straight out of Farragut Academy, a Chicago high school, in 1995, and the Timberwolves did start playing better once they got him. After years of reeking, they made the playoffs for the first time in Garnett's second season.

A lucky guess, some might say.

But what about Marbury? More than a month before the 1996 draft, Lordan told that same *Pioneer Press* columnist, "I see the Wolves getting the fourth pick."

A few days later, she was ridiculed by a *Minneapolis Star Tribune* columnist because the way the NBA draft lottery was set up, the Timberwolves could not draft fourth overall. Based on the Timberwolves' final regular-season record, it was mathematically impossible for them to have that fourth pick.

Then came draft day. The Timberwolves had the fifth pick. They used it to select Ray Allen.

Then the Timberwolves traded Allen and a future first-round pick to the Milwaukee Bucks for Stephon Marbury, who had been the fourth pick in the draft.

The psychic was right.

Go back to her comment. Lordan never said the Timberwolves would draft fourth. She said she saw the Timberwolves "getting the fourth pick."

And Marbury was the fourth pick.

Soon after Marbury became a Timberwolf, Lordan made an in-your-face telephone call to the *Star Tribune* columnist.

The next thing you know, there will be sightings of vampires, alien life forms, and benevolent oil company executives.

HOCKEY

WHO WAS THE CHEAPEST OWNER IN MINNESOTA SPORTS HISTORY?

63

When it comes to skinflint owners of Minnesota teams, there's plenty of competition for the top spot.

Take Calvin Griffith. He is sort of the patriarch of Minnesota's penny pinchers. Ol' Calvin never met a nickel he didn't want to hoard.

The Twins never would have existed if Calvin hadn't believed there was more money to be made in Minnesota than in Washington, D.C. He packed up the Senators and made them the Twins in 1961.

The Twins led the American League in attendance their first ten seasons in Minnesota, so there was some money for Griffith to pocket. It never was enough, though. Griffith was, as former Twins manager Tom Kelly called him upon his death in 1999 at age 87, "one of the dinosaurs of the game." And these dinosaur owners believed in paying their players as little as possible.

One time, Hall of Fame slugger Harmon Killebrew and Griffith were $500 apart on a new contract. Griffith refused to budge. Killebrew budged. He told Griffith that if the $500 meant that much to the old coot, he would go ahead and sign the contract so he wouldn't miss spring training.

The advent of free agency in the 1970s turned Griffith into baseball's leading tightwad. In 1982, he was bombarded with criticism after trading catcher Butch Wynegar and pitcher Roger Erickson to the New York Yankees for a nobody infielder, a couple of minor leaguers, and cash. Was he getting good players? It didn't seem like he cared—all Griffith was doing was dumping salaries and adding cheap, no-talent players just to make the bottom line look prettier.

Two years later, Griffith dumped the team. He sold it to Minneapolis banker Carl Pohlad for $36 million.

And the Twins went from one miserly owner to another.

How cheap was Pohlad? Well, he was known for bringing his own bananas to breakfast at a hoity-toity restaurant.

He didn't become a billionaire by giving money away, which is something many Twins who played for him can attest. Desperate for a new stadium financed primarily by Minnesota's taxpayers, Pohlad always kept a tight lid on salaries. Even after getting public financing for a new stadium that would be constructed in Minneapolis, Pohlad told his underlings to stick to a strict budget. To his credit, Pohlad hired two terrific baseball men who often made the tight finances work—Andy MacPhail and Terry Ryan.

But Pohlad's love of money was most evident during several flirtations with out-of-state buyers. He didn't care if he upset fans. He only cared about making a buck.

Even with all of this, though, Pohlad wasn't the tightest of wads in Minnesota's history.

Neither was Red McCombs, who ranks right up there in this corner of the world among cheapskate owners. Almost from the day he purchased the Vikings, McCombs whined that he needed a new, state-financed stadium. When he didn't get one, he sold the team. And the word is, on the day of the sale, he had someone collect all the petty cash in the team's front office.

But that still doesn't make a guy the cheapest owner. That title (as well as that of most-reviled owner in the history of Minnesota sports) is earned by one Norm Green.

He's the guy who hijacked the North Stars from Minnesota and dropped them in Dallas because of—what else?—the lure of more money.

Green, one of the largest commercial real estate developers in his native Canada, seemed like a decent enough fellow when he first bought the North Stars in 1990. He would stand in the concourse at Met Center and hand out neckties with the team logo on them to season-ticket holders. Then people got to know what he was really all about.

Green went to the city of Bloomington and asked for money to add more seats to the Met Center, which was located right next to where the old Metropolitan Stadium had been in Bloomington. The city didn't ante up, so that became one of Green's excuses to pack up the franchise. He never really considered moving the North Stars into Target Center in Minneapolis, even though that would have made sense, and the North Stars could have remained a Minnesota team. But Green wanted out of Minnesota. He was more interested in making cents than sense—millions upon millions of cents. He even looked into moving the North Stars to Anaheim before Dallas became his landing zone.

Many Minnesotans also believe Green wanted to hightail it out of the state because his executive assistant filed a sexual harassment suit against him and he wanted to put distance between himself and those claims. He settled out of court for a reported $1 million.

Nowadays, Norm Green is remembered as Norm Greed. On northstarhockey.com, a website dedicated to North Stars fans, there's still plenty of anger over the way Green yanked the franchise out of Minnesota in 1993: "Not since the departure of the Brooklyn Dodgers has there been anything in sports history to match the measure of this cruel separation between a franchise and its many long-time fans."

Toward the end of his carpetbagging tenure in Minnesota, North Stars fans would chant "Norm Green sucks!" at games. They did this for a simple reason.

It was true.

WHO WAS MINNESOTA'S BEST HOMEGROWN HOCKEY PLAYER?

64 Jordan Leopold was a terrific hockey player for the University of Minnesota. He was so good he won the Hobey Baker Award as a senior in 2002 and led the Gophers to their first NCAA men's hockey championship in 23 years. He was a Minnesota kid, born and brought up playing hockey in the state.

But he's not Minnesota's best homegrown hockey player.

Neal Broten played on the 1980 U.S. Olympic team and starred for both the University of Minnesota and the Minnesota North Stars of the NHL. Born in Roseau, he is the only player ever to be a member of teams that won an NCAA championship, an Olympic gold medal, and the Stanley Cup.

He's not Minnesota's best homegrown hockey player, either.

Here's a hint: It's not a guy.

Krissy Wendell is the answer. She's the one. She's No. 1.

Long before she became Minnesota's best homegrown hockey player and one of the most dominant hockey players in the world, Wendell was a standout baseball player. In 1994, as a 12-year-old, she was just the fifth girl to take part in the Little League World Series. She was the catcher for her

Brooklyn Center Little League team.

Krissy began skating when she was two years old, but her parents wouldn't let her play hockey until she turned five. Her parents tell the story of her exclaiming, on her fifth birthday, "I can play now!"

She was a wonderful baseball player, but she was even better in hockey. She proved that time and again in high school, collegiate, and international competition. In high school, she scored 335 points in 62 games, and that included playing one season on the boys' team. She scored 219 goals her final two seasons, and was named Ms. Hockey for Minnesota after leading Park Center High School to a state title as a senior.

While helping lift the University of Minnesota women's hockey team to national titles in 2004 and 2005, Wendell was voted the Western Collegiate Hockey Association Player of the Year both seasons. In 2005, when she led the WCHA with 43 goals and also had 58 assists, she won the Patty Kazmaier Memorial Award that goes to the best player in women's college hockey.

Wendell played on two U.S. Olympic-medal winning teams, and captained the 2006 Olympians to a bronze medal. She played in five world championships through 2006, leading the U.S. team to the world title in 2005 with a tournament-best nine points.

Krissy Wendell wasn't just good. She was as good as they come.

BESIDES MARIO, WHO HURT THE NORTH STARS IN THE 1991 STANLEY CUP FINALS?

65 Ever watch *The Honeymooners* with Jackie Gleason as Ralph Kramden? There's a memorable scene where Ralph realizes he got himself in big trouble over something he said. So, he bellows to his wife, Alice, "I've got a big mouth!"

Members of the 1991 North Stars had big mouths, too, and it sure didn't help them when they faced the Pittsburgh Penguins in the 1991 Stanley Cup Finals.

One thing you don't want to give to an opposing team looking for any kind of an edge is bulletin-board material. The North Stars said stuff during the best-of-seven series that didn't just find the way to the Penguins' bulletin board. They said enough to wallpaper the Penguins' locker room.

The Penguins became upset when they read in the *St. Paul Pioneer Press* that several North Stars already were talking about visiting the White House and President George H.W. Bush after winning the Stanley Cup. While the Twins visited the White House after winning the 1987 World Series, championship teams don't always get to pay a visit to the president, and it was more of a rarity in the NHL than other sports because so many Stanley Cup champions over the years have been Canadian teams.

"I love George! I love Dan Quayle! I love that whole administration! Tell (Bush) I'd love to go," North Stars defenseman Chris Dahlquist said. "We've got all kinds of Americans on our team. The winner of this series should go."

"Tell George (Bush) I'm a Canadian, but that I'd still try to vote for him. Count me in," fellow North Star Basil McRae said.

"It would be an honor," North Stars forward Neal Broten said. "Most championship teams get to go. I guess it's just a matter of getting an invitation. It would be nice if either Pittsburgh or us got an invitation."

The Penguins chose to overlook Dahlquist saying, "The winner of this series should go" and Broten saying, "It would be nice if either Pittsburgh or us got an invitation." No, the Penguins focused on the audacity of the North Stars even bringing up a White House visit. Well, there were a few other things, too.

"We heard they had books out to look at (championship) rings, too," said Peter Taglianetti, one of the Penguins. There also was talk of victory parades. "It makes them look silly," Taglianetti said.

Another Pittsburgh player, Troy Loney, told a Pittsburgh writer, "It ticks you off, really. One guy says this. One guy says that. It's like, why should we bother playing? You could only take so much of that."

The North Stars did get a little ahead of themselves. All those things were being said when they only held a 2–1 series lead.

"Did you see it? Did you see it?" Penguins coach Bob Johnson said to a writer after seeing what the North Stars were saying. "They're planning their parade. I thought it was best-of-seven."

It was. And the Penguins made sure the North Stars knew it, winning the next three games to claim Lord Stanley's chalice.

Mario Lemieux was the star of that series with the North Stars, with 5 goals and 7 assists despite sitting out Game 3 with back spasms. He easily won the Conn Smyth Trophy that goes to the playoffs MVP. He hurt the North Stars, to be sure.

But the North Stars hurt themselves, too. Just like Ralph Kramden, they had big mouths!

WHO HAD THE MOST JAW-DROPPING, EYE-POPPING GOAL EVER FOR A MINNESOTA TEAM?

66 Dino Ciccarelli could put the puck in the net. He scored more than 50 goals in two different seasons with the North Stars and, one year, tallied 45 goals for them. He could be dazzling on the ice, but was he the one who scored the most jaw-dropping, eye-popping goal of all?

Nope.

Neither did Bobby Smith, the legendary North Star.

Neal Broten had plenty of options, having played for the North Stars, the University of Minnesota, and the 1980 U.S. Olympic team, which practically was a Minnesota team. But it wasn't Broten, either.

Was it Marian Gaborik of the Wild? Again, nope.

All those guys just mentioned scored impressive and important goals. But the goal worthy of the most jaw drops, eye pops, head shakes, and double takes was scored by a freshman at the University of Minnesota.

Oh, he was a good freshman. So good that he was just finishing up high school when the New York Islanders chose him with the seventh overall pick in the 2006 NHL Entry Draft.

Anyone who follows hockey in Minnesota probably knows his name without being told but, just in case, it's Kyle Okposo. And he did something that you almost had to see to believe.

In a game against Minnesota State in December 2006, Okposo scored a between-the-legs goal. Now, you will see a lot of goals slipping between a goaltender's legs. But Okposo actually shot the puck between his own legs.

Okposo was skating from the right side and heading toward one side of the net when he took a pass from teammate Ryan Stoa in the first period of a 1–1 game. Mike Zacharias, the Minnesota State goaltender, was protecting that corner of the net. It appeared Okposo's best chance for a goal was to skate past him and try to poke the puck into the other corner, and it looked as if that was just what Okposo would try to do.

Zacharias did what any savvy goaltender would do. He moved with Okposo so he could be in position to block the shot.

When Zacharias moved, Okposo went into jaw-dropping, eye-popping mode. In a quick, deft motion, he used his stick to slide the puck between his legs and shove it past Zacharias. If you only saw the stick, you would have thought some other player had reached it under Okposo's crotch to take a shot.

It was such an impressive goal that a local TV station had Okposo later duplicate it several times after a practice. The

Islanders also showed footage of the goal against Minnesota State between periods of a game to let their fans get a look-see at the type of player who would one day be playing for them.

To listen to Okposo tell it, there was no other shot he could make. He called it "instinctive."

Others would call it jaw-dropping and eye-popping.

WHO WERE THE FIVE BEST SCORERS ON MINNESOTA'S NHL TEAMS?

67 Well, we only have the North Stars and Wild to choose from, so let's get started. Here they are, in descending order, along with trivia related to each of them that you can use to stump others . . .

5. BILL GOLDSWORTHY

Goldsworthy was the North Stars' first star offensive player, and quite the goal scorer. After a few games with the Boston Bruins, Goldsworthy joined the North Stars in 1967 and, before long, was their most dangerous scorer. Starting in the 1969–70 season, Goldy scored more than 30 goals in five of the next six seasons for the North Stars. Chosen to play in five NHL All-Star games, his best season came in 1973–74 when, in 74 games, he had 48 goals and 26 assists for 74 points. Goldsworthy's trivia: What was the name for that dance move Bill Goldsworthy did to celebrate a goal? Answer: The Goldy Shuffle.

4. BOBBY SMITH

The first overall pick by the North Stars in the 1978 NHL amateur draft, Smith had two stints with the franchise. He spent five full seasons with the North Stars at the start of his NHL career, then played seven seasons with the Montreal Canadiens before returning to Minnesota for three more seasons. While he won the Stanley Cup with the Canadiens in 1986, Smith was a member of the North Stars' two Stanley Cup teams that lost in the finals (1981 and 1991). Smith's best seasons with the North Stars came in his first go-round with them. In 1981–82, he had his finest season, when he scored 43 goals with 71 assists for 114 points. Smith's trivia: Which player scored more points than hockey legend Wayne Gretzky to win the Ontario Hockey League scoring title during the 1977–78 season? Answer: Bobby Smith, whose 69 goals and 123 assists for 192 points beat Gretzky's 182 points.

3. MARIAN GABORIK

The only Wild in this top five, Gaborik could some day ascend to the No. 1 spot. But first, he has to stay healthy for entire seasons. When not sidelined by injuries—he lost 34 games in a row to a groin injury during the 2006–07 season—

Gaborik was one of the NHL's most dangerous players. The third overall pick of the 2000 NHL Entry Draft, he had back-to-back 30-goal seasons in 2001–02 and 2002–03. Despite missing 17 games with a groin injury in 2005–06, Gaborik had 38 goals and 28 assists for 66 points in 65 games. If he can shake that injury bug, he can become one of the league's top scorers. Garborik trivia: Who scored the first goal as well as the first hat trick in Wild history? Answer: Marian Gaborik, who scored the first goal in October 2000 and the first hat trick in November 2001.

2. NEAL BROTEN

Broten won an NCAA championship with the University of Minnesota. He won an Olympic gold medal with the 1980 U.S. hockey team. And then he won over North Stars fans with his ability to score goals and generate points. While he also played for the Stars after they moved to Dallas, won a Stanley Cup with the New Jersey Devils, and played for the Los Angeles Kings, the bulk of Broten's career was spent with the North Stars (1980–93). In five of his seasons with the North Stars, Broten averaged more than a point a game. In his first full season (1981–82), he set rookie team records for goals (38), assists (60), and points (98). Broten's best season was in 1985–86, when he became the first American-born NHL player with 100 points. He had 29 goals and 76 assists for 105 points in 80 games that season. Like Smith, Broten was a member of the North Stars' 1981 and 1991 Stanley Cup teams.

173

Broten trivia: Who is the only hockey player ever to win an NCAA title, an Olympic gold medal, and the Stanley Cup? Answer: Neal Broten.

1. DINO CICCARELLI

Ciccarelli played for five teams during his 19-year NHL career, with nearly half of that time spent with the North Stars (1980–89). The best scorer in franchise history, Ciccarelli scored more than 30 goals in seven of his nine seasons with the North Stars. Four times he scored more than 40 goals, twice more than 50. Ciccarelli's best season was in 1981–82, when he had 55 goals and 51 assists for 106 points. But the 1986–87 season was just about as impressive; he scored 52 goals with 51 assists for 103 points. Ciccarelli scored 1,200 points in his NHL career, 651 of them with the North Stars. Ciccarelli trivia: What former North Stars player had a Topps rookie card that said he set two NHL playoff records after he "scored the most goals by a rookie with 14 and tallied the most points by a rookie with 21"? Answer: Dino Ciccarelli, and those stats came during the 1980–81 playoffs.

WHO'S ON MINNESOTA'S HOCKEY DREAM TEAM?
(Part I, Male Forwards)

68

There's just one rule for this argument: Members of the team have to be Minnesota natives.

Okay, there's also a second rule: To make the top three, a forward had to have a brilliant college and/or pro career in Minnesota.

The state has produced some terrific centers and wings, including Doug Woog, Aaron Broten, Pat Micheletti, Scott Bjustad, Corey Millen, and Johnny Pohl. They all were good, just not good enough to make the top three.

So here goes with the three best male forwards the state has produced:

3. BRIAN BONIN

Bonin, a White Bear Lake native, led the nation in scoring as a senior at the University of Minnesota with 34 goals and 47 assists for 81 points. That season, he was named first-team All America, Western Collegiate Hockey Association (WCHA) Player of the Year, and won the Hobey Baker Award. While at Minnesota, Bonin went to two NCAA Frozen Fours and played on Gopher teams that had a winning percentage of .660. Bonin's best years of success on the ice came while in college. He was drafted by the Pittsburgh Penguins, but played just five games with them during the 1998–99 season. He played seven games with the Wild in 2000–01 before heading overseas to play a couple of seasons with a professional team in Switzerland.

2. JOHN MAYASICH

A two-time, first-team All-America center for the University of Minnesota in 1954 and 1955, Mayasich was called "the Wayne Gretzky of his time," by his Gophers coach, John Mariucci. An Eveleth native, Mayasich holds the Gophers' scoring records with 144 goals and 298 points. He averaged an amazing 1.4 goals and nearly 3 points a game. Mayasich also holds the Gophers' single-game scoring records for most goals (6) and points (8). While a teenage boy in Eveleth, Mayasich led his high school team to four state championships. Mayasich never played in the NHL, but he did play on two U.S. Olympic teams, winning a silver medal in 1956 and a gold medal in 1960. Mariucci once said of Mayasich, "The words to describe the boy haven't been invented. When I say he's the best, that's totally inadequate."

1. NEAL BROTEN

Broten came down from Roseau and set the Gophers' freshman scoring record with 50 assists while leading the Gophers to the 1979 NCAA title. He left after his freshman year to play for the gold-medal winning 1980 U.S. Olympic team, and returned for a sophomore season during which he had 17 goals and 54 assists for 71 points. As a sophomore, Broten became the first recipient of the Hobey Baker Award that goes annually to the player voted that year's best in college hockey. Broten played from 1981–97 in the NHL, including 11 seasons with the North Stars. He became the first American with 100 points in an NHL season, and was the first hockey player to be on teams that won an NCAA title, an Olympic gold medal, and a Stanley Cup championship. Broten was a key member of the New Jersey Devils' 1995 Cup-winning team.

WHO'S ON MINNESOTA'S HOCKEY DREAM TEAM?

(Part II, Male Defensemen and Goaltender)

69 This argument still has just those two rules: Dream Team members have to be Minnesota natives, and, as with the forwards, they had to have a brilliant college and/or pro career in Minnesota.

Mike Ramsey, Mike Crowley, and Todd Richards were exceptional defensemen, and just missed making the cut. As for goaltenders, Jack McCartan, Adam Hauser, and Kellen Briggs were very good, just not as good as the pick here.

Here are the two best male defensemen, and then the best goaltender the state has produced:

2. JORDAN LEOPOLD (DEFENSE)

The day after receiving the Hobey Baker Award in 2002, Leopold led the Gophers to their first NCAA national title since 1979. A senior that season, Leopold set the school record for a defenseman with 20 goals and finished with 48 points. His 45 career goals are the most by a University of Minnesota defenseman. A Golden Valley native, Leopold was only the Gophers' fourth two-time All American and the first in school history to win the Hobey Baker Award and an NCAA title in the same season. Drafted by the Calgary Flames, Leopold played three seasons with the Flames before moving to the Colorado Avalanche for the 2006–07 season.

1. JOHN MARIUCCI (DEFENSE)

You can't leave the godfather of Minnesota hockey off the Dream Team. Before he became the Gophers' coach in 1952 and helped popularize the sport even more than it already was in the state by stocking his team with Minnesota lads—"This is a state institution and should be represented by Minnesota boys"—Mariucci was a first-team All America defenseman who led the 1940 Gophers to an undefeated season and the AAU national championship. After his college playing days were over, Mariucci became one of the few Americans in the Canadian-dominated NHL and spent five seasons with the Chicago Blackhawks. In his first season as the Gophers' coach, Mariucci took a team that had been 13–13 the previous season to a 23–5 record and the NCAA championship game. Best-known as a coach and for his grassroots approach to promoting hockey in Minnesota, Mariucci's outstanding career as a player sometimes is overlooked.

ROBB STAUBER (GOALTENDER)

The first goaltender ever to win the Hobey Baker Award, Stauber was just a sophomore at the University of Minnesota when he was presented with college hockey's highest individual honor. During that 1988 season, the Duluth native started in all of the Gophers' 44 games, had a school-record 5 shutouts, and held a 2.72 goals-against average. He was a first-team All American that year, and still holds single-season Gopher records for games played, minutes played, saves, and shutouts. While the Gophers' goaltender, the University of Minnesota went to three straight NCAA Frozen Four tournaments and won back-to-back WCHA titles. Stauber had a 73–23 record in three seasons with the Gophers before moving on to play in the Los Angeles Kings' organization. He also played six games with the Buffalo Sabres in 1994–95 before ricocheting around in the minor leagues. He returned to his alma mater to coach the Gophers' goaltenders in 1999. He was the goaltender coach when the

Gophers won back-to-back NCAA titles in 2002 and 2003 and held that position through the 2006–07 season.

WHO'S ON MINNESOTA'S HOCKEY DREAM TEAM? (Part III, Women Only)

70 Girls and women haven't been playing hockey in Minnesota anywhere near as long as the boys and men. Though the history isn't long, it is impressive.

Here are the five best women hockey players with Minnesota roots, regardless of position:

5. RONDA CURTIN (FORWARD/DEFENSE)

This high school superstar from Roseville began her career at the University of Minnesota as a forward but switched to defense as a junior. At Roseville, Curtin won multiple state titles and, in 1999, was Minnesota's Ms. Hockey winner. She set a state high school scoring record with 465 points that was broken by her younger sister, Renee, who had 544 points in the 2000–01 season. Renee suffered head injuries in high school that prevented her from playing college hockey. Meanwhile, Ronda helped the Gophers become national champions in 2000.

4. WINNY BRODT (DEFENSE)

After helping the University of New Hampshire win a national championship in 1998, Brodt transferred to her home state to play for the University of Minnesota. A Ms. Hockey Award winner, she led Roseville High School to an undefeated season and a state title. Brodt was a key member of the Gophers' national championship team in 2000. She made the 2006 U.S. Olympic team that won a bronze medal.

3. JENNY POTTER (FORWARD)

A member of three Olympic teams (1998, 2002, 2006), Potter played college hockey at Minnesota-Duluth after transferring from the University of Minnesota. At Minnesota-Duluth, Potter, who calls Eagan home, was a three-time, first-team All America selection (1999–2000, 2002–03, and 2003–04). Potter scored 108 goals with 148 points for 256 career points while with the Bulldogs. At the Olympics, she earned gold (1998), silver (2002), and bronze (2006) medals.

2. NATALIE DARWITZ (FORWARD)

Besides making her debut with the U.S. National team at the age of 15, Darwitz scored 170 goals for the Eagan High School varsity girls team as a seventh and eighth grader. A two-time member of the U.S. Olympic team, she won a silver medal with the 2002 team and a bronze in 2006. Darwitz also was a member of the University of Minnesota's back-to-back national championship teams in 2004 and 2005. In 2005,

Darwitz scored 102 points, the most by any man or woman hockey player in NCAA Division I college history.

1. KRISSY WENDELL (FORWARD)

One of the world's best players, Wendell helped the University of Minnesota win its back-to-back national titles after leading her Park Center High School team to a state title as a senior. She was voted the WCHA Player of the Year twice and, in 2005, won the Patty Kazmaier Memorial Award that goes to the best player in women's college hockey. Wendell played on two U.S. Olympic-medal winning teams and was captain of the 2006 team that won a bronze medal.

HIGH SCHOOL, COLLEGE, OR PRO, WHO ARE MINNESOTA'S TOP HOCKEY COACHES?

To make this list, you don't have to have been born in Minnesota, or even have played hockey in the Land of 10,000 Lakes. You just have to have coached in the state, and done a pretty impressive job of it, too.

Here are Minnesota's top five hockey coaches:

5. JACQUES LEMAIRE

Lemaire is one of the best coaches in the NHL, maybe even the best, and this Quebec native will go higher on this list if he takes the Wild to a Stanley Cup championship, something he did with the New Jersey Devils in 1995.

4. WILLARD IKOLA

The goaltender on two NCAA national championship teams at Michigan in 1951 and 1952 as well as a member of the 1956 U.S. Olympic team that won a silver medal, Ikola did his coaching at the high school level. In a 33-year career that touched five decades (1958–91), Ikola took his Edina teams to the state tournament 19 times and won eight state championships. He had just one losing season, his first as a coach, while amassing a state-record 616 victories. His overall record was 616–149–38. In 1990, he was inducted into the U.S. Hockey Hall of Fame in his hometown of Eveleth.

3. DON LUCIA

The University of Minnesota coach since 1999, Lucia won national titles in 2002 and 2003 to become just the fourth NCAA coach ever to win back-to-back hockey championships. His 2006–07 Gophers held the No. 1 ranking in the nation for most of the season. Lucia, 47 when the 2006–07 season began, annually has the top high school players in the land coming to play for him and he has a chance to exceed Herb Brooks' school-record three NCAA titles with the Gophers.

2. JOHN MARIUCCI

Already a legend in the state for his play as a defenseman with the Gophers, who he led to the AAU national title in 1940, Mariucci expanded his legend status as the University of Minnesota's coach. He compiled a coaching record of 193–130–15 from 1952 to 1966, with a break in 1956 to coach the U.S. Olympic hockey team to a silver medal in Italy. More important than his record was Mariucci's devotion to growing the sport of hockey in Minnesota. He did that by filling his Gopher teams with Minnesota boys. "If they're not quite as good as some Canadians," Mariucci said, "we'll just have to work a little harder, that's all."

1. HERB BROOKS

Brooks coached the University of Minnesota to three national titles (1974, 1976, 1979) before guiding an upstart bunch of mostly college boys to a stunning run at the 1980 Olympics that didn't end until they had won the gold medal and etched themselves into history as the Miracle on Ice.

OUTDOORS

IS FIGURE SKATING A SPORT AND ARE THE SKATERS ATHLETES?

72 Minnesotans love winter sports: ice hockey, downhill skiing, cross country skiing, and curling. They love ice fishing, snowmobiling, and broomball, too. And they really love watching the top athletes in the world compete in those sports every four years when the Winter Olympics roll around.

That started way before the 1980 U.S. Olympic hockey team, which was stocked with Minnesota players and had a Minnesotan as its coach when it shocked the world (especially the Soviets) and won the gold medal.

In just about every Winter Olympic sport, you will find a Minnesotan. They've competed at the Olympics in ice hockey, long-track speedskating, short-track speedskating, curling, luge, bobsled, biathlon, and every type of skiing you can name.

And if there are Minnesotans competing in Olympic sports you can bet there will be other Minnesotans watching them compete.

Minnesotans also love watching figure skating, even though it isn't a sport, and the skaters aren't athletes.

Ice skating is packaged like a sport and the skaters are athletic, but come on. You don't get to call yourself an athlete or what you do a sport when you have to wear makeup and sequins and buy hair spray by the pallet.

And that's just the guys.

Figure skaters are no more athletes than ballroom dancers or race car drivers. Just because something takes athleticism and some physical skill doesn't mean it's a sport. Juggling tennis balls or even chainsaws takes a certain amount of vigorous movement and talent, but that doesn't make juggling a sport.

And let's not even get started on ice dancing. Those kids wear even more makeup and sequins than figure skaters. They're the ones who couldn't cut it as figure skaters, so they team up with somebody of the opposite sex and sashay around the ice.

Just like figure skating, ice dancing is fun for some people to watch. And just like figure skating, it's not a sport and the ice dancers aren't athletes.

WOULD MINNESOTA ROADS BE FRIENDLIER WITH FEWER BICYCLISTS?

73 The trouble started with Greg LeMond. He won the Tour de France in 1986 and became the first American ever to conquer that bicycle race. Suddenly, Minnesota roads started getting clogged with men and women of every size and shape pedaling away in their too-tight Spandex biking outfits.

The number of cyclists on Minnesota's roads increased even more after 1989 and 1990, when LeMond, who lives in the Minnesota community of Medina, won back-to-back Tour de France races.

When LeMond was done, somebody else came along to fuel this cycling obsession. Lance Armstrong won seven of the darn Tour de France races in a row, causing a run on Spandex outfits and racing bikes in Minnesota and elsewhere.

But we're not concerned with elsewhere . . . just Minnesota.

Now, to be clear: There are plenty of Minnesotans who like to ride bikes on trails meant for bike riding. The folks on these bike trails aren't a problem, because they're on bike trails.

It's some of the wannabe LeMonds and never-will-be Armstrongs that can make your blood percolate. These bicyclists don't believe in using bike trails. Oh, no. They believe they have a right to pedal on the same roads used by cars and trucks. And they do—to a point.

The ones who obey the rules of the road are tolerable.

It's the other ones, the scofflaw cyclists who run red lights and ignore stop signs and refuse to yield, who make some people want to wrap them and their ultra-light carbon fiber bikes around the nearest tree. Road rage isn't always confined to the driver of one motor vehicle wanting to kick the ass of the driver of another motor vehicle. Sometimes, it involves a motor vehicle and a SOB (spandex-obsessed bicyclist) who thinks he owns the frickin' road.

Imagine you're driving along in your gas-guzzling SUV or fuel-efficient hybrid car and suddenly, up ahead, there is one of these packs of law-breaking cyclists. You can't get around them because they're hogging the road by riding four or five abreast. So, you're stuck going way slower than you should be, trying to figure out which rule of the road they're going to break next. They somehow got it into their heads, which are usually protected by helmets equipped with tiny side mirrors, that they can make their own rules on the road.

Well, they can't!

They should just get off the damn road.

WHO'S MINNESOTA'S GREATEST GOLFER?

74

You can make a case for Tom Lehman. In 1996, he won the British Open after several years of being considered the best golfer in the world never to win a major. That same year, this Austin-born, Alexandria-raised Minnesotan was named the PGA Tour Player of the Year. Lehman had won five PGA Tour events through 2006, played in two Ryder Cups, and was the non-playing captain for the U.S. Ryder Cup team in 2006.

But it's not him.

And it's not Tim Herron. Nicknamed Lumpy because he has a build that is, well, lumpy, Herron had four PGA Tour wins and no victories in a major through 2006. Born in Minneapolis and raised in Wayzata, Herron is south of Lehman on the list of Minnesota's all-time best golfers.

This isn't a trick question, either. We're not going to proclaim somebody as Minnesota's greatest golfer just because that person happened to be born within state borders. So, if you're thinking it's Lee Janzen, two-time U.S. Open winner and eight-time PGA Tour winner through 2006, uh-uh, it's not him, either.

Janzen's tie to Minnesota is that, like Lehman, he was born in Austin. Janzen didn't grow up in Minnesota. His childhood years were spent in Baltimore and Florida. But even if he spent his entire life in Minnesota, Janzen still wouldn't be Minnesota's greatest golfer.

Here's a hint: Minnesota's greatest golfer isn't a man.

It's Patty Berg, one of the greatest golfers of all time, male or female.

Berg, who died in September 2006 at the age of 88 from Alzheimer's disease-related complications, won an LPGA Tour record 15 major titles.

Read that last line again. Those 15 titles were just in LPGA major tournaments. She had 60 victories overall.

A Minneapolis native who attended the University of Minnesota, Berg was one of the 13 founding members of the LPGA Tour in 1950, and was the tour's first president from 1950–52.

Before helping put together the LPGA, Berg won the 1938 U.S. Women's Amateur, the 1946 U.S. Women's Open, and was a seven-time winner of both the Titleholders Championship and the Women's Western Open. The Titleholders was a prestigious women's event held in Augusta, Georgia, at the Augusta Country Club. Like its male counterpart, The Masters, which took place at Augusta National Golf Club, it was considered a major tournament.

Berg was the Associated Press's Female Athlete of the Year three times (1938, 1943, 1955) and a member of both the LPGA Tour and World Golf Halls of Fame. In 1978, the LPGA began offering the Patty Berg Award, which goes to people who make outstanding contributions to women's golf. She won the award herself in 1990, raising the question: Why didn't she get it sooner?

Berg wasn't just tough to beat on a golf course. She was tough, period. During World War II, she served as a lieutenant for three years in the U.S. Marine Corps.

One of the great sidebars to Berg's life is that she once played quarterback on a sandlot football team that included Minneapolis neighbor and friend Bud Wilkinson, who would become one of college football's most successful football coaches ever at Oklahoma.

So, Patty Berg couldn't just hit a ball. She could throw one, too.

But it was her ball-striking ability with a golf club in her hand that gained Patty worldwide fame and made her Minnesota's greatest golfer.

WHO WAS THE MOST SUCCESSFUL RACE HORSE WITH MINNESOTA TIES?

75 If we break it down to the last quarter century, or even the last half century, it's no contest. Unbridled was the most successful race horse with a Minnesota connection. Owned by Minnesotan Frances Genter, Unbridled won the 1990 Kentucky Derby and the Breeders' Cup Classic.

He also finished second in the Preakness Stakes that year, and received the Eclipse Award that goes to thoroughbred racing's best three-year-old colt. Unbridled was a fine horse, the best Minnesota-owned thoroughbred ever, but not the most successful race horse ever linked to Minnesota.

That would be Dan Patch.

Dan Patch wasn't a thoroughbred, though. He was a standardbred. He didn't race with a jockey on his back. He pulled a cart called a sulky, and he competed in a sport known as harness racing. And he wasn't just the best in Minnesota. He was the best anywhere, and he was a superstar in his day. Granted, his day was a long time ago. Dan Patch did his racing around the turn of the century—the turn from the nineteenth to the twentieth century.

Owned by Minnesota native Marion Savage for most of his

life, Dan Patch resided in Minnesota from the time Savage purchased him as a six-year-old in 1902 until his death in 1916. Savage died a day later, and it has been said the cause of death was grief over the loss of his wonder horse.

Harness racing was far more popular at the turn of the twentieth century than it is now, and Dan Patch was famous even before Minnesota became his new home. Born in Indiana, he began racing as a four-year-old, and when he was sold to New Yorker M.E. Sturgis in 1900, he "was already recognized as a horse of unusual potentials and the sum paid for him by Mr. Sturgis set a record at that time," according to the Dan Patch Historical Society. In his career, Dan Patch broke world records no fewer than 14 times. He held 9 world records when he retired. Dan Patch never lost a race and, in 1906 at the Minnesota State Fair, he lowered the world record for a mile to 1:55, a record that stood for more than 50 years.

Crowd estimates put the number of people who saw Dan Patch run at the State Fair in 1906, and also in 1903 and 1905, at 80,000 to 100,000. As Jim Anderson noted in a 2005 story about Dan Patch for the *Minneapolis Star Tribune*, if those estimates were right "they remain the largest crowds to witness a sporting event in Minnesota."

Anderson also wrote that "a little boy named Harry Truman wrote (Dan Patch) a fan letter, and young Dwight Eisenhower fondly remembered seeing him at the Kansas State Fair."

Dan Patch was so popular that his name was linked to endorsements for everything from cigars to stoves and washing machines, and he had a street named after him at the State Fairgrounds—Dan Patch Avenue. To top it off, in 1949, a movie was made called *The Great Dan Patch.*

Dan Patch also brought fame to Marion Savage, and the Minnesota city of Hamilton, where Savage lived, was renamed Savage.

Dan Patch wasn't just a great Minnesota horse. He was the greatest horse ever to take part in harness racing, and that gives him the nudge over Unbridled.

COLLEGE/
HIGH SCHOOL

WAS GLEN MASON A GOOD COACH?

76 Jim Wacker was a nice man but a lousy coach. Yeah, he did OK at places like Texas Lutheran and Texas Christian, but he flopped in the big time. He couldn't recruit in the Big Ten, and he couldn't win in the Big Ten. And when he was fired as coach at the University of Minnesota after the 1996 season, the Gophers football program was a mess.

Glen Mason changed that. He did at Minnesota what he had done at Kent State and Kansas. He made the program respectable.

Following six straight losing seasons, the Gophers under Mason traveled to seven bowl games and amassed a 123–121 record.

Mason had some nice wins along the way: beating No. 2-ranked Penn State 24–23 in State College, Pennsylvania, in 1999; putting away sixth-ranked Ohio State 29–17 in Columbus, Ohio, in 2000; and knocking off Michigan 23–20 for the first time in sixteen seasons in 2005, and at Ann Arbor, no less.

But, overall, Mason's Big Ten record was miserable—32–48. Under him, the Gophers' highest finish in the conference was fourth place, and all those bowl games he took them to were second rate. There was the Micronpc.com Bowl, the Wells

Fargo Sun Bowl, the Music City Bowl (three times), and the Insight Bowl.

Mason had a decade to lift the Gophers to that upper echelon and failed. The best season he had at Minnesota came in 2003, when the Gophers went 10–3. It should have been better. It would have been better if the Gophers hadn't blown a late 21-point lead over Michigan. It wasn't the first time a Mason team frittered away a lead, and it wasn't the last.

There always seemed to be some sort of psychological blockage with Mason's teams that kept them from figuring out how to handle success.

Mason never quite figured out how to handle his running backs, either, and he had some impressive ones. Marion Barber III and Laurence Maroney were among the best backs in college football, finishing among the national leaders in rushing yardage in the early and mid-2000s. The thing is, Mason rarely used them in the passing game. It was such a waste of talent. Both were used far more extensively as receivers once they got to the NFL. When asked why he didn't throw more to his backs, Mason usually shrugged and downplayed the importance of expanding their role.

Meanwhile, throughout his time at Minnesota, Mason whined that the football facilities were substandard for a Big Ten program. The training room and locker room never were big enough. The coaches' offices and meeting rooms were cramped. Playing at the Metrodome was a recruiting detriment. That last issue was addressed when state legislators voted in

2006 to build a new 50,000-seat stadium on campus.

Mason wanted a new stadium. Unfortunately, he won't be around to coach the Gophers in it when it is completed in 2009.

That inability to put teams away is what ultimately cost Mason his job. The Gophers led Texas Tech by thirty-one points in the 2006 Insight Bowl, but lost in overtime.

Two days later, Mason was fired.

Mason was a good coach. He just wasn't good enough.

The Gophers need somebody better, somebody to take them to that next level. Somebody to bring them Big Ten titles and put them in BCS bowl games.

IS THE GOPHERS' NEW FOOTBALL STADIUM GOING TO BE BIG ENOUGH?

77 Let's cut right to the chase. The answer is no. The Gophers' new 50,000-seat football stadium will not be big enough, not when there are three Big Ten stadiums—Michigan's, Ohio State's, and Penn State's—that seat more than twice the fans the University of Minnesota's TCF Bank Stadium will.

Now, some people will argue that a 50,000-seat stadium is plenty big enough when you consider how few people attended Gophers games at the Metrodome. In more than two decades of playing at the Dome, the Gophers rarely drew more than 50,000 fans in games that didn't involve border rivals Iowa or Wisconsin, who always brought along thousands of fans.

The Gophers' best crowds were in the early and mid-1980s, when they averaged more than 50,000 in 1982, 1984, 1985, 1986, and 1987. There was an initial surge in attendance when the Dome was something new, and then nationally known coach Lou Holtz brought in big crowds in his two seasons at Minnesota (1984–85). Fans kept coming the following two years, but attendance began to drop off after back-to-back mediocre seasons.

The folks who think that the stadium's plenty big enough also will argue that if the need for more seating becomes apparent, the new stadium could be expanded to hold 72,000 to 80,000 fans.

Here's the problem: Only Northwestern's Ryan Field, which seats 47,130, will be smaller than the Gophers' new place. So, every other team in the Big Ten, particularly those three with 100,000-plus seating, will ask recruits, particularly those from Minnesota high schools, if they really want to play in a pint-sized stadium.

For most kids, particularly young boys just entering adulthood, the perception is that bigger is better.

So, when the Gophers' new stadium opens in 2009, it will be big enough to hold the fans. But it won't be big enough to grab a hold of many of the recruits other Big Ten teams are interested in.

DID ANYTHING GOOD COME OUT OF THE GOPHERS' CHEATING SCANDAL?

78 The academic cheating scandal at the University of Minnesota was a bad thing ... a very bad thing.

Jobs were lost.

Careers were ruined.

When the *St. Paul Pioneer Press* broke the story in March 1999, the initial reaction around Minnesota was anger. The story opened with an explosive lead that claimed at least twenty members of the men's basketball team had, as the paper put it, "research papers, take-home exams or other course work done for them during a five-year period, according to a former office manager in the academic counseling unit who said she did the work."

At first, the anger wasn't directed at the Gophers. It was aimed at the newspaper. The *Pioneer Press* was accused of sensationalizing a story as the Gophers were preparing to play their first game in the 1999 NCAA tournament.

The vitriol subsided in time, replaced instead by disgust that cheating actually did take place at the university.

As mentioned in the last question, that former office

manager-turned-whistleblower was a 50-year-old woman named Jan Gangelhoff, who estimated for the *Pioneer Press* that she did more than 400 pieces of course work from 1993 to 1998 for members of the basketball team. Players from the Gophers' 1996–97 Final Four team were implicated.

The scandal rocked the university to its core.

Coach Clem Haskins, athletics director Mark Dienhart, and vice president of student development and athletics McKinley Boston all would leave their jobs.

However, some good did come out of the scandal.

It was an awakening for the university. For years, Gophers basketball coach Clem Haskins had his own fiefdom, and he was able to run the program without interference from administration officials. It was in that lax environment that cheating occurred.

University officials reviewed how things were being handled throughout the athletics department, and out of that came a termite's determination to make sure something like a cheating scandal would not happen again. That's a good thing.

Immediately after the story broke, several key players incriminated in the cheating scandal were benched and not allowed to play in the first round of the NCAA tournament against Gonzaga. The depleted Gophers team lost to Gonzaga, which used that win as a springboard to advance even deeper into the tournament.

In an interesting twist, the coach hired to replace Haskins

was Dan Monson, who was Gonzaga's coach and probably would have been ousted in the first round of the NCAA tournament if the Gophers had a full squad.

Saddled with NCAA sanctions for years, Monson was unable to return the Gophers' basketball program to the national prominence it enjoyed in the late 1990s. Monson was fired early in the 2006–07 season because the program still wallowed in mediocrity.

What Monson did do, and never received proper credit for doing from university officials or fans, was restore integrity to Gophers basketball.

And that's another good thing . . . a very good thing.

WAS ANYTHING FUNNY ABOUT THE GOPHERS' CHEATING SCANDAL?

79 The University of Minnesota men's basketball program was rocked when a cheating scandal was uncovered in 1999.

Head coach Clem Haskins, who just a few seasons earlier had been named the top college basketball coach in the nation, lost his job in the fallout. The athletics director as well as others in the athletics department also left the university in the aftermath of the academic fraud, which was disclosed by the St. Paul Pioneer Press in a series of stories that won the newspaper a Pulitzer Prize.

The basketball program was in ruins after the NCAA stepped in and levied sanctions that lasted several seasons. It was not a happy time on the Minnesota campus. But, as stand-up comedians will tell you, humor can be found anywhere, even in pain and suffering.

And there was some humor to be found amid the Gophers' scandal.

The whistleblower who admitted to writing papers for basketball players was a woman named Jan Gangelhoff. She told the Pioneer Press she wrote more than 400 "pieces of course work for players" from 1993 to 1998. Gangelhoff also said that, toward the end of her writings, she began giving players course work related to topics that interested her.

So, players were turning in papers on topics such as eating disorders.

OK, that's not so funny. It's conceivable a strapping young basketball player would have an interest in writing about eating disorders. He might have a friend or relative struggling with anorexia or bulimia or compulsive overeating.

Players also handed in papers about women's advancement in the workplace.

Again, that's not so funny. They may have been sensitive to the plight of working women struggling to get ahead for so many years.

Another paper turned in by members of the Gophers'

men's basketball team had to do with the *menstrual cycle*.

It's too bad Gangelhoff didn't write a first-person account of what it's like to give birth and provide that to these 6-foot-something young men to turn in as their own work.

That would have been worthy of an F-plus.

WHAT WAS THE ODDEST THING A MINNESOTA ATHLETE EVER DID? (COLLEGE DIVISION)

80 Randy Moss took a lot of heat from fans and members of the media when he made believe he was dropping his drawers at Lambeau Field. Likewise, leaving the field before a game was over wasn't exactly what you'd call a bright idea on his part.

Yeah, Moss did some goofy things. But he did them in the NFL. He was a professional goofball. His antics don't count here. We're only considering loopy behavior by college athletes.

Tyler Hirsch climbed the charts with what he did during the 2005 WCHA Final Five.

Hirsch and the University of Minnesota hockey team had just lost to Colorado College when Hirsch went over to an official and asked for a puck. The official gave him one, unaware of what was to come.

His teammates already were headed into the locker room, also unaware of Hirsch's plans.

Hirsch put the puck at center ice and took off skating toward the net with it. He shot the puck into the net. Okay, that's a strange thing to do after you've just lost a game and there are no players on the ice.

But Hirsch wasn't finished. He then hurled his body into the net.

Then he got up, headed back to center ice, and laid down his stick. After that, he headed for the exit.

Even his coach called what Hirsch did "bizarre." Hirsch took some time off from the team, then returned. And then left again: In January 2007, with the Gophers ranked first in the nation, Hirsch was thrown off the team by coach Don Lucia. Hirsch was a talented offensive player, but he's likely to be remembered even more for his odd behavior after that game.

You know who did something even odder than Hirsch? Mitch Lee.

Lee also was a talented athlete. His game was basketball. He played for the Gophers in the mid-1980s, and his career ended abruptly after he was charged with rape. It was the second time he was charged with that crime while a member of the Gophers' basketball team.

Lee was acquitted both times. He didn't return to the team after the second acquittal.

But after that first acquittal, Lee was so excited he decided to celebrate. A lot of people celebrate with champagne. That's what Mitch Lee did . . . sort of.

In his first game back with the Gophers after the acquittal, Lee trotted onto the court in a great mood. He had a champagne glass shaved into the side of his head.

Nobody said, "Cheers." Nobody cheered.

The people who weren't picking their jaws up off the floor just stared in disbelief. They had just seen the oddest thing an athlete at a Minnesota college ever did.

BESIDES BUD GRANT, WHICH MINNESOTA COACH SHOULD HAVE SOMETHING NAMED AFTER HIM?

81 Putting Bud Grant's name on the new Vikings' stadium would be nice, but that's unlikely. There are too many millions of dollars for the Vikings to make by selling naming rights. At the very least, the Vikings should name their practice facility after him . . . or the road in front of the new stadium. Or, better yet: Bud Grant Field at Whichever-corporation-buys-naming-rights Stadium.

Putting Bud's name on something should be a no-brainer, and he's not the only Minnesota coach who deserves his name on something. There's a University of Minnesota coach who should be honored that way, too.

Over the years, the university has shown an inclination to name buildings and arenas after former coaches.

There's the Bierman Building, which houses the athletics administration offices on campus. It is named after Bernie Bierman, the football coach who guided the Gophers to five undefeated seasons and national titles in 1934, 1935, 1936, 1940, and 1941.

There's Williams Arena, where the Gophers play basketball. It's named after Dr. Henry L. Williams, who coached the Gophers football team from 1900–21. He had five undefeated seasons and just two losing seasons. Though Williams didn't coach basketball, university officials chose to honor him when the original arena was remodeled in 1950.

The basketball version of Williams was L.J. Cooke, who coached the Gophers for 27 seasons (1897–24) and led them to national titles in 1902 and 1919. In 1938, the university named its then-new athletics administration building Cooke Hall, which today is home to the School of Kinesiology & Leisure Studies as well as offices for recreational sports.

There's also Mariucci Arena, where the hockey team plays. It is named after John Mariucci, who is credited with fostering the growth of youth and high school hockey in Minnesota because, while hockey coach at the university from 1952–66, he relied on Minnesota players. An All-America hockey player at Minnesota in 1940 and an NHL player for five seasons, Mariucci is in the United States Hockey Hall of Fame and the Hockey Hall of Fame.

The original Mariucci Arena was adjacent to Williams Arena, but when a new hockey arena was built in 1993 the name was switched over. The old Mariucci Arena was converted from a hockey rink into a 5,700-seat sports pavilion, where volleyball games as well as gymnastics and wrestling matches are held.

The sports pavilion is called just that—the Sports Pavilion. That's the place that should be renamed some day.

And the name on it should be J Robinson's. (That's really his first name, just J with no punctuation mark.)

Robinson is one of the most successful college wrestling coaches in America. He has turned the Gophers into a national power, repeatedly winning dual matches and tournaments right there in the Sports Pavilion. He took over the program in 1986 and led it to several NCAA National Duals titles and national championships.

During the 2006–07 wrestling season, Robinson guided the Gophers to their second straight National Duals championship and fourth in seven years. It's a prestigious title awarded to the team that is the last one standing after several rounds of matches against the top programs in the nation.

Heading into the 2007 NCAA tournament for individual

wrestlers and teams, Robinson already had won national team titles (2001 and 2002) and coached eight wrestlers to national titles. In a nine-year stretch that began in 1997, Robinson coached the Gophers to eight top-three finishes in the NCAA tournament. It was the most by any wrestling program in the nation over that period.

Robinson has done for the wrestling program what Bierman once did for the football program and Mariucci did for the hockey program: bring it national prominence.

When he's done coaching, something should be named after J Robinson . . . something like the Sports Pavilion.

WHO'S THE LEAST-KNOWN SUCCESSFUL COACH THE GOPHERS EVER HAD?

82 Like it has done to ancient civilizations, time also has a way of burying people and making them little more than a historical footnote.

That has happened to L. J. Cooke. Ever heard of him? Well, maybe you have if you've read the argument about which University of Minnesota coach should have something named after him. Cooke already has his name on a building. In 1938, Cooke Hall became the university's new athletics administration building. Nowadays, it houses the School of Kinesiology & Leisure Studies and offices for recreational sports, as well as the Tucker Center for research on girls and women in sport.

Cooke got his name on that building because of what he did: construct the Gophers' basketball program pretty much from scratch.

The Gophers began playing basketball in 1895, but there was no coach and they played mostly YMCA teams for two seasons. Cooke came along in 1897. He had been the physical director at the Minneapolis YMCA, which, by the way, beat the coach-deprived 1895 Gophers twice. Anyway, Cooke was hired in 1997 to run the university's physical education department and oversee the new gymnasium. He also became the Gophers' basketball coach that year.

He held the job for 27 seasons.

Over that span of nearly three decades, Cooke coached the Gophers to national titles in 1902 and 1919, as well as three Big Ten titles in 1911, 1917, and 1919.

The NCAA didn't exist until 1906 and didn't offer a national title in basketball until 1939. Cooke's two teams were national champions, though, winning the prestigious title awarded at that time. His 1902 team went 15–0 and won the Helms Athletic Foundation national championship, while his 1919 team went 13–0 and won the Helms national title once again.

Cooke's 247 victories are a record for a basketball coach at Minnesota. His .656 winning percentage, based on a

247–129–2 record, is the best in Gophers basketball history for a coach who lasted five or more seasons. The only Gophers coach with a better winning percentage was Bill Musselman's .683 mark, but he was at Minnesota only four seasons before bolting to coach the San Diego Sails in the American Basketball Association.

Cooke is the only Gophers basketball coach to ever win a national title in basketball.

Sadly, no successful Gophers coach, regardless of the sport, has faded so deep into obscurity.

DOES MINNESOTA'S HIGH SCHOOL LEAGUE CROWN TOO MANY CHAMPIONS?

83 In regard to high school football in Minnesota, it makes sense to have more than one state champion. After all, it would be silly to have a nine-man team from a school with only a few dozen boys play against, say, Eden Prairie High School, which has more than a hundred eager lads come out for football every year.

But, even in football, the Minnesota State High School League is awarding way too many state titles. Besides having a game to decide a nine-man champion, there also are state championship games, based on the size of the schools, for Class A, Class AA, Class AAA, Class AAAA, and Class AAAAA.

Yep, there are six state champions in football.

Some of those classes should be consolidated, but we live in a society with too many adults determined to make as many kids as possible feel special. Some youth leagues don't even keep score so every kid can feel like a winner. That's not the way the real world works, and awarding multiple state championships in the same sport is not the way Minnesota's high school league should be operating.

Minnesota's state hockey tournament used to be something truly unique. Teams from all across the state—from the big, the small, and the really tiny schools—all competed in a postseason that didn't conclude until one team was left . . . a single state champion. Then the state hockey tournament got diluted. It was broken into two classes. Guess what—it was better the other way.

Basketball is also divvied up into classes, four in fact, which means four state champions. That's three too many. Basketball used to crown just one state champion; that's how it was done from 1913 to 1970. One of Minnesota's most memorable state championship teams was the 1960 Edgerton bunch that came from a tiny city with a population of just 961 people. These kids were Minnesota's version of Hoosiers. Edgerton beat a much bigger school from Austin 72–61 and, at the time, *Minneapolis Tribune* columnist Charles Johnson wrote, "Edgerton's state championship basketball team must go down in history as one of the most amazing organizations that ever set the pace in the prep parade. No more popular victory ever was registered in this classic."

In wrestling, there are three individual state champions in each weight class. Why do they need to have Class A, Class AA, and Class AAA champions in wrestling? It's one kid on the mat against another kid. School size doesn't matter. The state wrestling tournament would be a lot more exciting if the best wrestlers from each of these classes met to decide one champion. Of course, then there would be fewer kids feeling special, and wouldn't that be a horrible thing?

One high school sport in Minnesota that has been doing it right and awarding just one state championship has been Nordic skiing. Oops. Maybe we shouldn't go broadcasting that. Somebody will think it's high time to start having multiple state champions in that sport as well.

WHAT MINNESOTA COACH WOULD YOU WANT YOUR KIDS TO PLAY FOR?

84

In professional sports, you will find a lot of ball-breaking coaches, and who has a problem with that? Most pro athletes are being paid damn good money, so they should be expected to produce. When they don't, they deserve a kick in the pants.

But you'll come across demanding coaches at every level, right on down to Little League. At all those levels, there is a fine line between pushing the right buttons with an athlete and being an A-hole. Some coaches know how to walk that line. Others don't have a clue.

Bud Grant was a Hall of Fame coach who took the Vikings to four Super Bowls. Tom Kelly was the Twins' manager both times they won the World Series. Jacques Lemaire won a Stanley Cup with the New Jersey Devils and was considered one of the NHL's best coaches when he took over the Wild. All three had reputations for being a hard-ass without being an A-hole.

The same could be said for the likes of Bill Musselman, Herb Brooks, and Glen Mason when they coached at the University of Minnesota.

But would you want your kid to play for somebody like that?

Or, would you want them to play for a coach who doesn't believe in whistles? A coach who encourages his players to call him by his first name? A coach who doesn't insist his players take part in a weightlifting program?

In other words, a coach like John Gagliardi.

Gagliardi has been the football coach at St. John's University for more than half a century. Since he got into college coaching in 1949, Gagliardi has won more games than any other coach in college football history.

And he's done it his way, a way that's appealing to athletes and their parents.

Gagliardi turned 80 in November 2006 and, just like it had been back in 1949 when he was coaching players who had fought in World War II and were older than him, he was still telling his players to call him John instead of Coach.

Gagliardi never cared how other coaches ran their programs. What he always cared about were his players. So, there were no blocking sleds or tackling dummies. There was no tackling during practice. No one wore pads during practice, just shorts or sweats. No practices lasted longer than ninety minutes.

Instead, Gagliardi taught his players the fundamentals of blocking and tackling and he gave them the right plays to run.

And it worked.

Besides all the wins, Gagliardi won four national championships. And more important than the wins and the titles, generations of parents sent their sons to play for Gagliardi. Some of these sons would play for Gagliardi, go on to have sons of their own, and send them to play for Gagliardi.

Every year, more than 150 players show up for the Johnnies' first day of practice. Most of them stay in the program, even though many know they'll never get to play.

"I'll tell you what I don't like about coaching: The guys whose hearts you break," Gagliardi told the *St. Paul Pioneer Press* in November 2006. "The guys who don't make the travel squad. The guys who don't get in the game. They can't all be all-conference or All-American. They can't even all be starters."

Maybe those players do it because they get something just as important as playing time. They get to be around John Gagliardi, a great coach who doesn't like to be called Coach.

DID GENETICS MAKE MIKE GRANT THE COACH HE IS TODAY?

85 Well, yeah, genetics plays a part in Mike Grant's overwhelming success as the football coach at Eden Prairie High School. Like his dad, Hall of Fame coach Bud Grant, Mike's brain is hotwired to know how to coach a team to victories.

While Bud did it at the professional level with the Vikings, Mike has become the most successful high school football coach in Minnesota over the past decade. In November 2006, he led Eden Prairie to its fifth state championship in 11 years in the class that features the state's biggest schools.

When Mike first took over at Eden Prairie, the Eagles had won three games over the previous three seasons. They won their conference in his first year as coach, and the wins just kept coming.

Every year, more than 200 kids try out for the various freshmen, sophomore, junior varsity, and varsity teams at Eden Prairie. That gives Grant a lot of talent from which to choose to keep right on winning.

Though his father certainly had an influence, Bud Grant wasn't the most influential coach in Mike Grant's career. That would be John Gagliardi, Mike's college coach at St. John's

University. Mike was a tight end, just like his dad, and helped the Johnnies win the NCAA Division III national championship in 1976. He also coached under Gagliardi.

"I think who you play under or coach under is your great influence," Mike Grant said.

Bud Grant rarely has offered advice or plays to Mike. There was this one time before the 2006 state high school championship game when Bud drew up a play for Mike to use. Father and son were deer hunting a few days before the big game and Bud left the play on the table for Mike to see.

"I didn't see it sitting there," Mike said. "He asked me if I saw it. I said, 'I missed it.' We'll get it in next year for him. We'll call it Bud Right or Bud Left."

Mike Grant often is asked why he hasn't gone into college coaching, or tried making it as a professional coach. When the University of Minnesota was doing its search for a coach to replace Glen Mason for the 2007 season and beyond, Grant said he was interested. However, the Gophers weren't interested in him. Elevating a high school coach to a major college program would take out-of-the-box thinking and be considered a ballsy move. The Gophers just weren't up for that.

Some day, Mike Grant may wind up coaching at some college somewhere. Maybe it will be one of Minnesota's NCAA Division III schools. His name has been mentioned for years by St. John's alumni as the guy who should replace Gagliardi when, or if, he retires. Then again, it's no lock Grant will do anything other than coach Eden Prairie to more state titles.

"If you let your ego get control of you, you think about (coaching in college or the NFL)," Grant said a few days after coaching Eden Prairie to its 2006 state title. "In the next month, 50 college coaches will come through here. There's one standing in the door now. To a guy, all of them want my job. They're on the road so much. They work 45 weekends a year. I don't know how you go hunting or fishing (working that much). If all those guys want my job, why should I leave it?"

Mike Grant has done at Eden Prairie what John Gagliardi has done at St. John's and what his father did with the Vikings: win . . . a lot.

THE GREAT, THE AWFUL, AND THE NEWSWORTHY

WHO BELONGS ON MINNESOTA'S MOUNT RUSHMORE OF COACHES/MANAGERS?

86 Never mind that bull about statistics being for losers. Statistics are for making a case about who belongs in the pantheon of Minnesota's greatest.

Here, in alphabetical order, are the three coaches and one manager and the stats that got them Mounted . . .

HERB BROOKS

He became a national figure after he led the U.S. Olympic hockey team to the gold medal in 1980, but Brooks was a highly successful coach before ever taking that bunch to Lake Placid to beat the Soviets in the semifinals and Finland in the championship game. Brooks coached at the University of Minnesota from 1972–79 and guided the Gophers to three national titles. After the 1980 Olympics, he coached four NHL teams, including the Minnesota North Stars, and won more than 200 professional games. In 2002, he became the U.S. Olympic coach once again, guiding the American team to a silver medal in Salt Lake City.

JOHN GAGLIARDI

Gagliardi became the football coach at St. John's University in 1953, and he kept right on coaching for more than half a century. His 2006 Johnnies finished the season 11–2 to raise his career coaching record to 443–120–11. He has more victories than any college football coach ever, and has won four national titles. Though St. John's is an NCAA Division III school, Gagliardi is recognized as one of the premier coaches in all of college football. The Gagliardi Trophy, which goes to the top Division III player in the nation each season, is named after him. In 2006, Gagliardi became the first active coach inducted into the College Football Hall of Fame.

BUD GRANT

Grant was the face of the Minnesota Vikings for 18 seasons. During that time, he coached the Vikings to eleven division titles and took them to four Super Bowls. Though the Vikings failed to win a Super Bowl, Grant's overall record of 168–108–5 and his ability to take teams to the big game helped get him elected to the Pro Football Hall of Fame. Already a successful coach in the Canadian Football League before joining the Vikings, Grant won 102 games with the Winnipeg Blue Bombers and is enshrined in the CFL Hall of Fame. Grant also was an outstanding athlete, starring in football, basketball, and baseball at the University of Minnesota. To top it off, he played professional basketball with the Minneapolis Lakers and pro football with the Philadelphia Eagles.

TOM KELLY

Kelly did what no other Twins manager could do. He led the Twins to world championships. In 1987, his first full season as manager, Kelly guided a team mixed with upstarts and veterans to a World Series victory over the St. Louis Cardinals in seven games. He and the Twins did it again in 1991, this time taking a seven-game series from the Atlanta Braves. Kelly retired following the 2001 season after 15 seasons as the Twins' manager. Though his career record of 1,140–1,244 was below .500, Kelly's teams went 8–2 in two League Championship Series. That, along with his two World Series titles, earn Kelly that spot alongside Brooks, Gagliardi, and Grant on Minnesota's Mount Rushmore of Coaches/Managers.

WHO BELONGS ON MINNESOTA'S MOUNT RUSHMORE OF ATHLETES?

87
You want great athletes? We got 'em, right here on Minnesota's Mount Rushmore of Athletes. Take a look, in alphabetical order, at the Big Four . . .

HARMON KILLEBREW

Known as "Killer," this compact first baseman from Payette, Idaho, hit 573 home runs in a career that spanned three decades. When Killebrew retired in 1975, only Babe Ruth had hit more American League home runs. In 22 seasons with the Washington Senators (1954–60), Minnesota Twins (1961–74), and Kansas City Royals (1975), Killebrew either tied or led the American League in home runs six times. He had 40 or more home runs eight times, and had 100 or more RBI nine times. In 1969, he won the AL's MVP award after leading the league in home runs, RBI, walks, and on-base percentage. He was elected to baseball's Hall of Fame in 1984.

GEORGE MIKAN

Mikan led the Minneapolis Lakers to five NBA championships in six seasons and revolutionized the way the position of center was played. After the 1950–51 season, the NBA widened the width of the foul lane from 6 to 12 feet because Mikan had used his 6-foot-10 body to dominate games inside the lane. His dominance continued even after the lane was widened. In a Hall of Fame career that lasted nine seasons, Mikan averaged 22.6 points and almost 10 rebounds a game. In 1950, the Associated Press named Mikan the best basketball player of the first half of the century.

BRONKO NAGURSKI

Nagurski is in both the College Football Hall of Fame and the Pro Football Hall of Fame. Before he became one of the NFL's first stars, Nagurski was an All-America player at the University of Minnesota in the late 1920s as both an offensive and defensive player. At 6-foot-2, 217 pounds, he had impressive size for the era in which he played college ball. He played tackle on defense, fullback on offense. He was tough to stop as a runner, and tough to run against. In a 1928 game against Wisconsin, his legend grew when he barged into the end zone with six Badgers clinging to him. In 1969, the Football Writers Association selected him as a tackle on the all-time All-America team. In nine NFL seasons (1930–37, 1943) with the Chicago Bears, Nagurski accounted for more than 4,000 yards and was named first-team all-NFL five times for his play as a fullback and linebacker. In 1943, after a five-year retirement, he helped the Bears win the NFL title. He was a charter member of both the College and Pro Football Halls of Fame.

KIRBY PUCKETT

Adored by fans and even members of the media, Puckett led the Twins to World Series championships in 1987 and 1991. He spent 12 seasons with the Twins (1984–95). Puck might have been there longer, but his career was abbreviated due to glaucoma and retina damage in his right eye. Puckett had a career batting average of .318 that, when he retired, was the highest for a right-handed hitter since Joe DiMaggio. He won the American League batting title in 1989 with a .339 average and had 2,304 career hits. He also was named to ten straight All-Star teams and was a six-time Gold Glove winner for his outstanding play in center field. Kirby Puckett was elected to the Baseball Hall of Fame in his first year of eligibility in 2001.

WHO WAS MINNESOTA'S ALL-TIME BEST ALL-AROUND ATHLETE?

88 Paul Bunyan isn't the only mythic character to come out of Minnesota. There also have been a few college and pro athletes who appeared larger-than-life.

In the late 1920s, there was Bronko Nagurski. He had a great name, and a great talent for trampling anyone in his way. This was back when he became a legendary figure for the University of Minnesota football team. The late 1940s and early 1950s belonged to George Mikan, the bespectacled giant who led the Minneapolis Lakers to five NBA championships in six seasons while revolutionizing the way the center position was played. The latter part of the twentieth century, well, that was Kirby Puckett's time.

Nagurski, Mikan, and Puckett all were great athletes. As for being Minnesota's all-time best all-around athlete, though, not a one of them was that.

Dave Winfield was better all-around. He starred for the University of Minnesota in basketball and baseball and was such a gifted athlete that he was drafted by four teams in three professional sports. The NBA's Atlanta Hawks and the ABA's Utah Stars drafted Winfield to play basketball.

Winfield didn't play football, but that didn't keep the Vikings from picking him in the 17th round of the same 1973 NFL draft in which they landed Chuck Foreman. Winfield's chosen sport, though, was baseball. He signed with the San Diego Padres and began a career that was so impressive you'll find his plaque in the Baseball Hall of Fame.

Winfield was something special as an athlete, but was he Minnesota's all-time best all-around athlete?

Uh-uh.

Minnesota's best-ever all-around athlete?

That would be Bud Grant. Yep, the Vikings' Hall of Fame coach also was one hell of an athlete.

Though he was born in Superior, Wisconsin, Grant will be forever linked with Minnesota. Even if he had never coached a game for the Vikings, Grant's imprint on Minnesota sports was ensured after starring in three sports for the Gophers and then playing for the Minneapolis Lakers.

Grant was able to play in both the NBA and NFL because he had the size and the skill. If he had given it a shot, he probably could have made it in pro baseball, too. There was a load of talent crammed into that 6-foot, 3-inch body.

The Philadelphia Eagles selected Grant in the first round of the 1950 draft, but he decided to stick close to home and play for the Lakers. He was a reserve on two of the Lakers' championship teams, and then switched to football. As a rookie, he led the Eagles in quarterback sacks. In his second season, he

229

was the NFL's second-leading receiver with 56 catches.

Rather than take less pay than he believed he deserved, Grant left the Eagles after just two seasons to play for the Winnipeg Blue Bombers in the Canadian Football League. He played both ways and was such an impressive team leader that ownership offered him the coaching job in 1956. He accepted it and, well, if you know anything about the Vikings you know that he did OK as a coach.

Nowadays, when people discuss Grant, it usually revolves around what he did as the Vikings coach. But, when you consider his career as an athlete—as Minnesota's all-time best all-around athlete—there's plenty more to talk about.

WHAT IS MINNESOTA'S MOST INFAMOUS SPORTS-RELATED SCANDAL?

89 For more than a quarter of a century, if you mentioned the Love Boat to anyone in Minnesota or anywhere else in America, it stirred memories of people with names like Julie McCoy, Gopher, Isaac, and Captain Merrill Stubing.

Nowadays, the Love Boat means something completely

different to Minnesotans. It's not a fond remembrance of something campy and fun, like the TV show that first aired in 1977. Instead, it's an ugly recollection of something sordid and salacious, words associated with athletes far too often these days.

The Minnesota version of the Love Boat is the state's most infamous sports-related scandal.

There have been individual athletes who got in trouble with the law, and the cheating scandal that took place with members of the University of Minnesota men's basketball team was a very bad thing. But nothing else that has happened in Minnesota involved anywhere near the decadence and lascivious details that increased the infamy quotient of the Love Boat incident.

On the evening of October 6, 2005, two party boats stocked with booze, strippers, and members of the Vikings left the docks at Al and Alma's Supper Club on Lake Minnetonka and cruised into infamy.

Things happened that night that were so far off the morality charts that Hennepin County Sheriff Pat McGowan said, "There was no shortage of inappropriate behavior on both boats."

McGowan spoke that piece at a December 2005 news conference to announce charges against four Vikings—quarterback Daunte Culpepper, cornerback Fred Smoot, offensive tackle Bryant McKinnie, and running back Moe Williams. Each was slapped with misdemeanor charges for indecent conduct, disorderly conduct, and lewd or lascivious conduct.

Though only those four players were charged, authorities estimated there were as many as 30 Vikings on those two party boats for a night of debauchery. About a week later, law enforcement officials told the *St. Paul Pioneer Press* they believed strippers who worked for an escort or call-girl service that catered to professional athletes were brought in from Atlanta, Florida, and other places to put all hands on more than just the deck.

According to crew members on the boats and the criminal complaints that emerged from those accounts, it wasn't too long after the boats shoved off that some of the women shoved their bodies into skimpy outfits or just got naked. The boats then reportedly turned into floating sex clubs. The criminal complaint alleged that McKinnie performed oral sex on women, and received it, too; Smoot used a sex toy on two women at the same time; and Culpepper and Williams received lap dances and fondled dancers. The charges came after interviews with party boat workers and an investigation by McGowan's office.

Word of the cruise spread across the nation and the Vikings became the punch line of Jay Leno jokes. Closer to home, Minnesotans were rightly outraged. The stories emerging from that night depicted athletes with no sense of civility and an arrogance that made them appear as if they believed they could do anything they wanted and get away with it because they were privileged as professional athletes.

None of the women were ever identified, and the players claimed the accounts were lies. Culpepper said he looked "forward to meeting my accusers in a court of law so they can be confronted with this lie. . . I didn't touch anybody and nobody touched me."

Smoot said of the charges, "That upsets me bad, because I didn't do anything on the boat."

Still, in May 2006, Smoot and McKinnie each agreed to pay $2,000 fines and perform 48 hours of community service for charges related to that October cruise. In April 2006, Williams was convicted of disorderly conduct, fined $300, and court-ordered to put in 30 hours of community service. Other than what it did to his reputation, Culpepper came out of the episode unscathed. Disorderly conduct charges against him were dismissed.

What never will be dismissed, at least in the memories of many Minnesotans, is how the Love Boat went from being a TV show to a show of unseemly behavior by members of the Vikings.

WHAT WERE MINNESOTA'S DARKEST DAYS FOR FAN BEHAVIOR?

90 It got ugly that December day in 1975 at the old Metropolitan Stadium, when Cowboys wide receiver Drew Pearson shoved Nate Wright and caught that Hail Mary touchdown pass to beat the Vikings' best team ever. Fans got angry and unruly. One of the fans threw a whiskey bottled that bonked official Armen Terzian in the head.

Oh, yeah. That was an ugly day.

It also was ugly in 1972, when a brawl broke out between University of Minnesota and Ohio State basketball players, and some fans decided to leave the stands and join in.

But it was even uglier over three evenings in late April and early May 2001, when Chuck Knoblauch, who helped the Twins win the 1991 World Series as a rookie, came back to the Metrodome for a three-game series as the left fielder for the New York Yankees.

Knoblauch was a fiery second baseman with the Twins, and fairly popular until he left the team after the 1997 season to join the Yankees. He had been a second baseman for the Yankees until that 2001 season, when he developed baseball's version of the yips. He suddenly had trouble making the throw to first base, which is why he was in left field on those dark days in 2001, the three darkest days ever for fan behavior by Minnesotans.

Generally, Minnesotans who attend games will boo and rant and occasionally even chant something catchy, such as "Norm Green Sucks." But what hundreds of them did to Knoblauch went beyond being rabid fans. They became thugs.

It started with the first game of the series on a Monday night. Early in the game, it was just verbal and visual abuse. Fans yelled derogatory comments at Knoblauch and some wore T-shirts showcasing a four-letter word that rhymed with Chuck. There also were 19 students from a local high school who wore T-shirts that spelled out, "Hey, Chuck, You Suck!"

Players learn to live with that sort of thing, and tolerate it. But then, in the 3rd inning, some of these thugs began hurling things at Knoblauch. Several dollars in coins whizzed past his head, as did a few bottles.

"There's no place for that stuff," Knoblauch said after the game. "I certainly didn't turn around and face them and take something in the eye. One bottle came pretty close after the (Doug Mientkiewicz) home run.

"People in the outfield tend to get a little crazy. It's great to have a section to root, but there's no place for being obnoxious and throwing things, regardless who's out there."

When the game ended, there were several thousand bottles

and cups hurled on the field. And it was a game the Twins won 2–1.

Over the next two games, it got even worse, as more thugs decided to show up and aim their venom and projectiles at Knoblauch. It didn't matter to these nut jobs that the Twins had more than doubled the number of security guards in left field from 6 on Monday night to 14 for the Tuesday and Wednesday night games.

By the time the three-game series concluded, Knoblauch had been pelted with coins, plastic bottles, golf balls, hot dogs, and other debris. The final game of the series was stopped twice because of objects thrown on the field, and a Twins official estimated more than 30 people had been eject-ed for hurling things at Knoblauch, who, luckily, wasn't struck.

After play was halted for eight minutes in the 6th inning because of all the crap thrown at Knoblauch, Twins manager Tom Kelly walked alongside Knoblauch into left field in an attempt to quell the unrest.

It worked . . . for a little while. In the 8th inning, more debris rained down..

After that final game of the series, Yankees manager Joe Torre called the behavior of these people "frightening."

It certainly was that.

WHAT IS MINNESOTA'S ALL-TIME BEST MASCOT?

91

It isn't T.C., the Twins' mascot who looks like a Sesame Street reject.

It isn't Regnar, the Vikings' wild-eyed, motorcycle-driving mascot who always looks like he's on his way to a rumble.

It isn't Crunch, the Timberwolves' trampoline-flying, shooting-shirts-into-the-crowd ball of fur who's named after a candy bar.

It isn't Goldy Gopher, another ball of fur who can be found racing around at University of Minnesota football and basketball games and skating between periods of Minnesota hockey games.

It isn't Vikadontis Rex, a short-lived Vikings mascot who looked like yet another Sesame Street reject.

It isn't even Hub Meeds, the original and most popular Vikings mascot who dressed up like a real Viking and patrolled the sidelines during the Purple People Eater days.

It is the pig—the St. Paul Saints mascot that really is a pig.

Every year, a different pig is used. It has to be done that way. Pigs have a reputation for, well, pigging out, so the mascot that begins the season as a piglet of about 20 pounds packs on the ol' weight at a rate of about a pound and a half a day. Eventually, that cute little piglet can turn into a real porker and weigh as much as 1,500 pounds. At that weight, they just get too big to haul to games and fulfill mascot duties. They lose their marketability and have more value at the market . . . the supermarket.

On their way to the Big Sty in the Sky, more than a few of the Saints' mascots have been introduced to the business end of a cleaver. It has been that way since Dennis Hauth and his wife, Marilyn, of River Falls, Wisconsin, began supplying the team with pork chops-in-waiting.

The pig mascots have been around as long as the Saints—a decade and a half. Only a few of them died of natural causes.

"We had Tobias die. He was the fourth mascot," Tom Hauth, Dennis and Marilyn's son, told the *St. Paul Pioneer Press*. "He died of a heart attack when he was ten months old. The original mascot, The Saint, died of old age. As the original mascot, it just didn't seem right to introduce him to the butcher block. He was like 6 ? years old when he left us. That's very old for a pig. He was down to about 1,300 pounds because he couldn't eat as much as he used to . . . He was about 4 ? feet tall and, when he stood up, he was eight to 10 feet long. He weighed more than the biggest pigs you see at the State Fair."

The 2006 mascot was named Bud Squealig. He was only eight weeks old and 20 pounds when he appeared on ESPN's Cold Pizza with Tom Hauth. Bud was preceded by mascots with names such as the Great Hambino, Hamlet, St. Paula, St.

Patrick, Squeal Diamond, Hammy Davis Jr., Kevin Bacon, Ham Solo, and Wilbur.

The first three mascots—The Saint, St. Paula, and St. Patrick—all rode a motorcycle. The motorcycle was custom built for the pigs, who were dressed in leather and strapped onto the, uh, hog.

Other mascots have been dressed in tuxedos and tutus, and even toted saddles and blow-up dolls to their backs. All the mascots are taught to deliver baseballs to the home-plate umpire between innings. It doesn't take extensive training. The only thing they really have to learn is to walk in the direction they're pointed.

The idea for a pig mascot came from the brainpan of Mike Veeck, one of the team's original owners and son of major league's baseball's all-time promotional wiz, Bill Veeck. One of Mike Veeck's other minor league teams had used a golden retriever to bring baseballs to the umpire, but a dog didn't make sense for the Saints.

A pig made perfect sense. St. Paul, after all, once was known as Pig's Eye. Besides that, pigs are naturals at hamming it up.

And hogging the spotlight.

92 The Lynx are a lucky bunch. That WNBA franchise, which plays at Target Center in front of paltry crowds, would have a lock on being the worst idea for a pro franchise in Minnesota history if not for one thing: the Fighting Pike. The Pike were an Arena Football League team that opened and closed shop in 1996.

The Pike just never caught on. Maybe it's because they never won a home game, going 0–7 at Target Center. Or it could be because Arena Football League teams work better in communities that don't have NFL franchises. Or perhaps it was that playing football on a converted hockey rink struck people as dopey.

The average attendance at Target Center was said to be nearly 8,900, but that figure, like the gear players wore on their shoulders, was padded. There were a lot of freebie tickets and, at some games, you would swear they were counting eyeballs instead of asses in the seats.

The Pike folded after the final game of the season, which was played against the Memphis Pharaohs in Tupelo, Mississippi. (Why Tupelo? It was because the Pharaohs had been evicted from their Memphis digs. Apparently the Pike wasn't the only Arena Football League team with problems.) Many of the people who worked for the Pike either didn't receive their final paychecks or they got checks that bounced.

About the only worthwhile thing the Pike did was produce this trivia question: Which well-known NFL kicker got his professional start kicking field goals and extra points for the Minnesota Pike?

The answer: Mike Vanderjagt, who made 2 of 6 field goals and 7 of 10 extra points.

WHAT WAS THE BIGGEST 12-MONTH PERIOD IN MINNESOTA SPORTS?

93 During an exciting April evening in 2003, the Twin Cities hosted playoff games for both the Wild and Timberwolves on the same night. While the Wild played the Vancouver Canucks in Game 3 of the NHL's Western Conference semifinals at Xcel Energy Center in St. Paul, the Timberwolves were facing the Los Angeles Lakers in Game 5 of the NBA's Western Conference playoffs at Target Center in Minneapolis.

It was a big night, though not a particularly enjoyable one

for the Wild and Timberwolves. The Wild lost to the Canucks to fall behind 2–1 in their best-of-seven series, although the Wild rallied to win the series in seven. Meanwhile, the Timberwolves lost to the Lakers to fall behind 3–2 in the best-of-seven series. They lost the next game and were out of the postseason.

Although there was quite a bit of civic pride in St. Paul and Minneapolis to have teams in playoff games on the same night, it was just one night in 2003.

Now, let's talk about the biggest year in sports in Minnesota.

It wasn't 1987, though that ranks right up there because the Twins won their first World Series and the 1987 Vikings reached the NFC Championship Game.

No, nothing beats that 11-month stretch bridging 1991 and 1992, when Minnesota hosted the Stanley Cup, which the Pittsburgh Penguins won in six games over the North Stars.

And the U.S. Open, won by Payne Stewart in an 18-hole playoff against Scott Simpson.

And the World Series, which the Twins won in seven games over the Atlanta Braves.

And the Super Bowl, which the Washington Redskins won by beating the Buffalo Bills 37–24.

And the men's Final Four, won by Duke 71–51 over Michigan.

Four World Series games in October 1991, the Super Bowl in January 1992, and the Final Four in early April 1992 all were played at the Metrodome. The North Stars played three games in the Stanley Cup finals at Met Center in May 1991. The U.S. Open was held at Hazeltine National Golf Club in Chaska in June of 1991.

Would it have been an even better year if the Twins weren't the only Minnesota team to win a championship? Of course, it would have been. But it still was some year.

As Frank Sinatra used to sing, it was a very good year.

WHY DO MINNESOTA ATHLETES GET IN SO MUCH TROUBLE?

94 Professional athletes are different than other people. They are more important than the rest of us. They have a special talent and that means they should receive special treatment. They deserve to make millions of dollars. They should be able to date any woman they desire. Laws, rules, and social mores should apply to normal folks, not to them. They are gifted and they are a gift to the world. Put another way, it's their world and we're just spectators in it.

Not every pro athlete thinks like that, but some do. Their minds become poisoned at a young age from all the coddling and adulation they receive from parents, coaches, friends, and even strangers.

And what happens as they grow older?

They misbehave.

Some just get into trouble with their team or the law. Some self-destruct. Let's take a look at Minnesota's history of both.

Perhaps the most infamous such Minnesota incident occurred in 2005, when four members of the Vikings got into hot water while on the water. These players had charges brought against them after taking a salacious ride on a party cruise soon dubbed the Love Boat. Offensive tackle Bryant McKinnie, cornerback Fred Smoot, and running back Moe Williams all paid fines and were court-ordered to perform community service, while quarterback Daunte Culpepper had disorderly conduct charges dismissed. Culpepper didn't get along with new coach Brad Childress and was traded, while McKinnie and Smoot played for the Vikings in 2006. The Vikings released Williams, but that had more to do with his age and production than his behavior. He signed with another team. Ultimately, the Love Boat incident damaged their reputations more than their careers.

In August 2006, safety Dwight Smith got into trouble after a preseason game when he and a woman were caught exchanging more than glances in a stairwell of a night spot in downtown Minneapolis. Both were cited for indecent conduct. Five months later, Smith pleaded guilty to the misdemeanor charge and was sentenced to 16 hours of community service, a $375 fine, and another $700 for what was described as prosecutor costs. He didn't lose his job or career over that.

He was more fortunate than a couple of other Vikings: Onterrio Smith and Koren Robinson.

Smith, who had a history of violating the NFL's substance abuse policy, was suspended for a year by the league and later released by the Vikings after getting caught at the airport with the "Original Whizzinator," a device that was developed to beat drug tests.

Robinson's career with the Vikings ended shortly after a drunk-driving arrest and a car chase in which police said speeds exceeded 100 miles per hour. Robinson already had a history of alcohol abuse.

And then there's Timberwolves forward Eddie Griffin. When he joined the Timberwolves in October 2004, Griffin brought with him a history of violence and alcohol abuse. In the early morning hours of March 30, 2006, Griffin drove his Cadillac Escalade into a parked sports utility vehicle. Eyewitness accounts and a lawsuit filed by the people leasing the SUV claim Griffin admitted to being drunk and that he was pleasuring himself while watching a porn movie on the DVD player mounted in his dashboard.

Then, in January 2007, the NBA suspended Griffin five games without pay for violating conditions of its anti-drug program. Griffin was killed in August 2007 when authorities say he ignored a railroad warning signal and drove his sports

245

utility vehicle into a moving freight train in Houston, Texas.

Minnesota's pro teams, particularly the Vikings and Timberwolves, have increased the odds of having players who get in trouble because they have been known to sign troubled players.

Both the Vikings and Timberwolves have been willing to take chances on players who come to them with baggage, and we don't mean a suitcase filled with clothes. To wit: Other teams had already given up on Robinson and Griffin when they landed in Minnesota. Furthermore, Onterrio Smith had a history of drug use in college, which caused him to slip to the fourth round in the 2003 draft. The Vikings are always on the lookout for a bargain, while Griffin was appealing to the Timberwolves because he came relatively cheap. The Wolves were paying Kevin Garnett around $20 million a year, so they had to bargain shop.

The Vikings were hoping Robinson and Smith would keep on the straight and narrow and steer clear on trouble. The Timberwolves had a similar hope with Griffin.

It didn't work out the way either team had hoped.

95

To make this list, an athlete didn't have to lose a limb, beat back death, or find salvation for his soul. What the athlete had to do was overcome a physical issue or imperfection, and then excel. By excelling, they were able to inspire others with issues or imperfections.

Here, in ascending order, are Minnesota's three most inspirational athletes:

3. RANDY FOYE

Some athletes play as if they don't have any heart. Randy Moss was accused of that when he loafed on plays or walked off the field before a game was over. With some people, you can't even find a heart if you look for it where it usually is. Timberwolves guard Randy Foye has a heart like that. Foye's heart doesn't beat on the left side of his chest, like most human hearts do. His heart is on the opposite side. So are his other vital organs. Foye came into this world with a condition known as situs inversus. All his internal organs are reversed, flip flopped from where you'll find them on most folks. The Timberwolves' first-round draft pick in 2006, whose exceptional play at guard during the 2006–07 season had Timberwolves fans and officials viewing him as the team's next great player, Foye is believed to be the first Minnesota athlete to have this condition, which occurs in about 1 in 8,500 people. While what he has is rare, Foye is an inspiration to all children who have had to deal with medical conditions that make them feel different or abnormal, that make them fear they won't be accepted or can't succeed because they're different.

2. GEORGE MIKAN

Back in the late 1940s and into the 1950s, the best thing that could have happened to kids with bad eyesight was George Mikan. As the center for the Minneapolis Lakers, Mikan was the best basketball player of his era . . . and he wore glasses. After that, it became a little easier and more acceptable for kids to wear glasses. It was less of a big deal. After all, George Mikan wore them and the kids could look through their glasses and see how great he played. Mikan led the Minneapolis Lakers to five NBA championships in six seasons. Counting the title the Lakers won in the National Basketball League, it was six in seven seasons. Voted the best basketball player in the first half of the century by the Associated Press, Mikan should go down in history as the most accomplished bespectacled athlete of all time.

1. KIRBY PUCKETT

Back in the 1980s and 1990s, Kirby Puckett was an inspiration for kids and anyone else who, like him, didn't have a sculpted body. While not what you'd call roly poly, Puckett had a short, thick physique. He was built like your plumber, or the guy who changes your motor oil. During his Hall of Fame career, Puckett showed everyone it doesn't matter how you look. It's how you perform that counts. And he performed wonderfully, leading the Minnesota Twins to World Series championships in 1987 and 1991.

WHO ARE MINNESOTA'S MOST ATHLETICALLY SUCCESSFUL SIBLINGS?

96 Well, for starters, there are the Carlson brothers. We're talking about the Carlson brothers from Edina—Bruce and Tim—who played hockey at the University of Minnesota in the early 1970s. Not the Carlson brothers—Jeff and Steve—who people know better as Jeff and Steve Hanson, who accounted for two thirds of the wacky Hanson brothers in the 1977 movie, *Slap Shot*.

Jeff and Steve were from Virginia, Minnesota, and they played hockey, but they're not quite what we're after here.

We're looking for siblings like the Hankinson brothers from Edina—Peter, Ben, and Casey—who each scored 100 or more points for the Gophers.

And brothers like Joe, Don, and Pat Micheletti from Hibbing. Each of the Micheletti boys scored more than 100 points for the Gophers. Pat scored 120 goals and had 269 points from 1983–86.

The Hankinson boys and the Micheletti boys were good, darn good, but they don't top our list.

Neither do Dan and Darby Hendrickson from Richfield. They both played at Minnesota, too, and Darby spent some time with the Wild.

Johnny and Tom Pohl from Red Wing aren't atop the list, either. Both played hockey at Minnesota. Johnny was captain of the Gophers' 2002 national championship team and went on to play for the Toronto Maple Leafs. Tom was a junior on the Gophers' 2006–07 team.

For sheer volume, it's tough to beat the Alm brothers from Minneapolis. Gary, Larry, Michael, and Richard all played hockey for the Gophers in the late 1950s and early 1960s, and a fifth brother, Tim, was the team's student manager.

But that isn't what we're going for, either.

What we want are siblings who stood head and shoulders (or head and shoulder pads, if they played football) above all others.

Bob and Pinky McNamara played football, and played it

real well, as halfbacks for the Gophers in the 1950s. They were from Hastings.

The Mauer brothers from St. Paul—Joe, Jake, and Billy—all played baseball in the Twins' organizations. Joe is the only one to make it to the majors, and he made it in a big way, winning the American League batting title in 2006.

Tim and Melissa Herron of Wayzata also had post-college success. Tim plays on the PGA Tour and Melissa is one of the top amateur women golfers in Minnesota.

The Herrons are right up there, with Krissy and Erik Wendell of Brooklyn Park as the most successful brother-sister combo from the state. Krissy led the University of Minnesota to national titles in women's hockey and became one of the top hockey players in the world, while Erik played hockey for the Gopher men's 2002 national championship team.

As for a sister combination, there's Ronda and Rene Curtin from Roseville, who were outstanding hockey players in Minnesota in the early 1990s.

Herb Brooks and his brother, Dave, were St. Paul kids who played hockey at the University of Minnesota, and one of them made a mark beyond college. As mentioned elsewhere, it had something to do with the 1980 Winter Olympics.

To be considered the most successful set of siblings in Minnesota, though, you have to have made a mark in high school, college, and beyond. And here, in ascending order, are the top three sets of athletically successful siblings from the Land of 10,000 (And Then Some) Siblings:

251

3. JIM AND KEITH FAHNHORST

A couple of brothers from St. Cloud, Jim and Keith both played in the NFL. After leaving the University of Minnesota in 1981, Jim played linebacker for two seasons in the United States Football League under legendary coach George Allen. In 1984, Jim joined the San Francisco 49ers as a free agent. He was a linebacker on three of the 49ers' Super Bowl championship teams (1984, 1988, 1989) and had 9 interceptions in his seven seasons with the franchise. Keith also played for the Gophers and the 49ers. He was an offensive tackle with the 49ers from 1974–87. During his tenure in San Francisco, Keith was part of the best and the worst teams in franchise history. Keith played on 49ers teams that went 2–14 in back-to-back seasons (1978–79) and he also was a member of the 49ers' first two Super Bowl championships.

2. BILLY, ROGER, AND GORDY CHRISTIAN

These three brothers grew up in Warroad. Gordy was the eldest brother. He played hockey at the University of North Dakota in the late 1940s and was a member of the U.S. Olympic team that won a silver medal in 1956. Billy and Roger were members of the 1960 Olympic hockey team that won the gold medal in Squaw Valley. Billy was the center on a line that had Roger as his left wing. In the first game of the medal round, Roger had a hat trick in a 6–3 victory over Sweden. Then, in a 3–2 upset win over Russia, Billy had two goals and Roger assisted on both of them. In the gold-medal game against Czechoslovakia, the U.S. trailed 4–3 after two periods, but the Americans scored 6 goals in the 3rd period to win 9–4. Roger had 4 goals in that game, including a hat trick in the third period. In 1964, Billy and Roger started Christian Brothers, Inc., and made hockey sticks that would be used throughout the world. In 1980, Billy's son, Dave, was a member of the Miracle on Ice hockey team that won the gold medal at the Winter Olympics in Lake Placid.

1. NEAL, AARON, AND PAUL BROTEN

Neal is the oldest and most famous of the Broten boys from Roseau. He's the only hockey player ever to play on teams that won NCAA, Olympic, and Stanley Cup championships. Broten won the NCAA title in 1979 with the University of Minnesota, where Aaron and Paul also played. He was a member of the 1980 U.S. team that shocked the Soviets in the semifinals and went on to win the Olympic gold medal at Lake Placid. During his NHL career (1981–97), Neal played for the North Stars, the Dallas Stars, the New Jersey Devils, and the Los Angeles Kings. He won the Stanley Cup with the Devils in 1995 in a four-game sweep of the Detroit Red Wings. Neal had 4 game-winning goals in the Devils' playoff run, including the Cup-clinching goal in Game 4 against the Red Wings. Aaron was Neal's linemate at Minnesota and had a 12-year NHL career that began during the 1980–81 season with the Colorado Rockies and ended in 1992 with the Winnipeg Jets. Aaron played a portion of the 1989–90 season with the North Stars. Paul, the youngest of the Broten bunch,

253

played in the NHL with the New York Rangers, Dallas Stars, and St. Louis Blues from 1989–96. How about that, having three brothers all playing in the NHL? That high level of accomplishment goes into why Neal, Aaron, and Paul Broten are Minnesota's most athletically successful siblings.

WHAT WERE MINNESOTA'S THREE BEST SPORTS-RELATED INVENTIONS?

97 Even without Thomas Alva Edison ever having lived in the state, Minnesota has been on the cutting edge of inventions over the years.

Minnesotans have given the world Scotch tape (as well as masking tape), the stapler, the bundt pan, and the world's largest ball of twine, which is 12 feet in diameter, weighs 17,400 pounds, and, for anyone interested, is rolled up in Darwin.

Here are the three best sports-related inventions to come out of Minnesota:

3. ROLLERBLADES

Rollerblades were invented by Minneapolis brothers and

hockey players Scott and Brennan Olson in 1979 as a way to simulate being on hockey skates when there's no ice available. In 1983, Scott Olson started Rollerblade, Inc. Rollerblades took off as an alternative to roller skates and became the first commercially successful in-line skate. For years, rollerblading was the socially acceptable term that referred to in-line skating no matter who produced the skates.

2. SNOWMOBILES

Other types of motorized snow vehicles had been around for years, but the modern-style snowmobile was first manufactured and mass produced by Polaris Industries in Roseau, Minnesota, in the 1950s. According to the official Polaris website, "The men who built the first Polaris snowmobile in December 1955 and January 1956 never claimed they invented the snowmobile. Others across the snowbelt were also trying to develop motorized snow machines. What the Polaris staff did, though, was build a snowmobile that really worked." In other words, they invented what evolved into the snowmobiles you see on trails today.

1. WATER SKIS

Yep, water skis were invented right here in Minnesota on Lake Pepin in aptly named Lake City. The inventor was an 18-year-old named Ralph Samuelson. In July 1922, Samuelson tried using barrel staves, then snow skis to successfully ski on water. Neither item worked. So, he went to a lumberyard and purchased two eight-foot-long boards that were nine inches wide. He boiled the tips of the boards to bend them. A few days later, he had his brother, Ben, tow him behind a motor-boat and, voila, water skis that worked. As you might imagine, the skis were rudimentary. Samuelson used leather strips for bindings and, as a ski rope, he bought 100 feet of window sash cord at a hardware store. According to the Water Ski Hall of Fame website, Samuelson "talked a blacksmith into making him an iron ring for a handle. He wrapped the ring with black tape to make it easier on his hands." Three years later, Samuelson put grease on a 4- by 16-foot ramp and did the first water ski jump. Can you think of a better place for water skis and water ski jumping to be invented than in the Land of 10,000 Lakes?

WHAT WERE MINNESOTA'S THREE BEST SPORTS-RELATED CREATIONS?

98 If something is innovative, it's either an invention or a creation. Rollerblades, snowmobiles, and water skis were inventions.

Here are Minnesota's three best sports-related creations.

3. CHEERLEADING

There was cheering way back in ancient times, like when people in the Roman Coliseum yelled in support of either the lion or the gladiator. But cheerleading, as it is known today, got its start November 2, 1898, at a University of Minnesota football game, when a group of students, led by an undergraduate named Johnny Campbell, stood in front of the crowd and led it in cheers. According to a university student publication that came out later that month, Campbell went with this cheer: "Rah, Rah, Rah! Ski-U-Mah! Hoo-Rah! Hoo-Rah! Varsity! Varsity! Varsity, Minn-A-So-Tah!"

2. PAUL BUNYAN'S AXE

The mythical lumberjack makes the list because of his association with college football, not because of the extremely tall tale that his footprints and those of his blue ox, Babe, created Minnesota's lakes. If there was no Paul Bunyan, there would be no Paul Bunyan's Axe to go to the winner of the annual football game between the Universities of Minnesota and Wisconsin. The Axe was introduced in 1948, but the results of games between the two schools dating to 1890 are printed on the axe's six-foot handle. Through the 2006 season, Wisconsin had won the axe 33 times to Minnesota's 23.

1. WHEATIES

Yeah, it's a food, but somebody had to come up with it; create it, if you will. And athletes have been known to eat and endorse the cereal made by Minnesota-based General Mills. According to the official Wheaties website, "The popular cereal flake in the orange box was born when a Minneapolis health clinician accidentally spilled some wheat bran mixture on a hot stove, creating tasty wheat flakes. The idea for whole-grain cereal flakes was brought to the attention of the head miller at Washburn Crosby Company (General Mills' predecessor), George Cormack, who perfected the process of producing the flakes. In November 1924, the ready-to-eat cereal known as Washburn's Gold Medal Whole Wheat Flakes during its development was ready for the market." Anyway, the name was shortened to Wheaties, and it became "The Breakfast of Champions."

WHAT TRAGIC DEATHS HIT MINNESOTANS THE HARDEST?

99 Here, in descending order, are the seven tragic deaths of sports-related figures that had the biggest impact on Minnesotans:

7. LYMAN BOSTOCK

A center fielder with the Twins for three seasons (1975–77), Bostock was shot and killed while in the backseat of his uncle's car in Gary, Indiana. The shooter didn't know Bostock. He allegedly was trying to gun down his estranged wife, who knew Bostock's uncle and had just met Bostock. Though he was playing for the California Angels when he was shot September 23, 1978, Bostock's death was felt by Twins fans who, just one season earlier, watched him finish second to Twins teammate Rod Carew for the American League batting title. Bostock was 27 when he died.

6. MALIK SEALY

A Timberwolves swingman and good complement to Kevin Garnett at the time, Sealy was on his way home from a birthday party for Garnett on May 20, 2000, when his sports utility vehicle was hit head on by a pick-up truck operated by a drunk driver going in the wrong direction. It was a senseless death, a death that reminded people just how precarious life is. Sealy was 30 when he died.

5. BILL GOLDSWORTHY

Though Goldsworthy's pro hockey career ended nearly two decades earlier, his death on May 29, 1996, touched Minnesotans and hockey fans throughout the United States and Canada because it stemmed from AIDS-related complications. In addition, Goldsworthy had been a popular player with the North Stars and one of its original members. In a February 1995 interview with the *St. Paul Pioneer Press*, Goldsworthy said there had been a three- to five-year period after he divorced his wife that he "wasn't as careful about sex as I should have been." Goldsworthy was 51 when he died.

4. BILL MASTERTON

A center who played just one season with the North Stars, Masterton was checked in a game against the Oakland Seals on January 13, 1968. He fell and struck his head on the ice at Met Center. He died two days later, the first and only player to die from injuries sustained in an NHL game. Masterton was 30 when he died.

3. HERB BROOKS

On his way back from a U.S. Hockey Hall of Fame celebrity golf event that included players who once played for him, the legendary coach of the 1980 U.S. Olympic hockey team died August 11, 2003, when the minivan he was driving rolled over on Interstate 35 in the northern part of the Twin Cities. Apparently not wearing a seat belt, his body was found 40 yards from his vehicle. Brooks was 66 when he died.

2. KOREY STRINGER

The 335-pound starting right tackle for the Vikings collapsed at training camp after throwing up three times during drills held in fierce humidity and temperatures that were in the 90s. He died in a hospital 15 hours later, on August 1, 2001, after having a body temperature of 108.8°F. Stringer's death hit Minnesotans so hard because he had been a healthy and strapping athlete in his prime, who left a wife and young child. Stringer was 27 when he died.

1. KIRBY PUCKETT

As mentioned previously, no death touched Minnesotans as Puckett's did. The most popular athlete ever in Minnesota, he died March 6, 2006, the day after suffering a stroke at his Phoenix home. Puckett was 45 when he died.

WHO ARE MINNESOTA'S HALL OF FAMERS OF TOMORROW?

100

An outstanding career isn't always enough to get an athlete into the Hall of Fame. Former Twins pitchers Bert Blyleven and Jack Morris are proof of that.

The Baseball Hall of Fame is the toughest to get into, followed by the Pro Football Hall of Fame, the Hockey Hall of Fame, and the Basketball Hall of Fame.

Here, in ascending order of their chances, are the five athletes on the 2007 rosters of professional teams in Minnesota who have the best shot of some day making it into their sport's Hall of Fame:

5. WILD FORWARD MARIAN GABORIK

First, Gaborik needs to stay healthy. Then he needs to do more than duplicate the 2005–06 season, when he scored 38 goals and 28 points in 65 games to average more than a point a game. He needs to exceed that type of production over several seasons. He also needs to lead the Wild to a Stanley Cup.

4. TWINS FIRST BASEMAN JUSTIN MORNEAU

Morneau makes this list on the strength of his 2006 season, when he won the American League MVP award with 34 home runs, 130 RBI, and a .321 batting average. Morneau will need another dozen or more seasons of 30-plus home runs, 100 and then some RBI, and .300 batting averages to get a serious crack at the Baseball Hall of Fame.

3. TWINS CATCHER JOE MAUER

Like Morneau, his friend and roommate, Mauer gets on this list primarily due to his 2006 season. Mauer became the first American League catcher ever to win a batting title when he hit .347 in 2006. He also became the first catcher to win a batting crown since Ernie Lombardi's .330 average won it in 1942 with the National League's Boston Braves.

2. FORMER TIMBERWOLVES FORWARD KEVIN GARNETT

In a dozen NBA seasons with the Timberwolves, Garnett already might have accomplished enough to earn entrance into the Basketball Hall of Fame. Though he hadn't won an NBA title and only reached the Western Conference championships once in his 12 seasons—he was traded to the Boston Celtics in the summer of 2007—Garnett averaged double figures in scoring and rebounding nine seasons in a row. KG and Hall of Famer Larry Bird are the only NBA players to

THE BEST MINNESOTA SPORTS ARGUMENTS

have 6 straight seasons averaging at least 20 points, 10 rebounds, and 5 assists.

1. TWINS PITCHER JOHAN SANTANA

He isn't there yet—there being a likely Hall of Famer—but Santana had the best shot of any twentysomething pitcher in baseball in 2007. Even though he was just 28 at the start of the 2007 season, Santana has already won two Cy Young Awards and finished third once. If he pitches another dozen seasons the way he performed from 2004–06, when his worst earned run average was 2.87 in 2005, Santana should reach 300 wins and collect a few more Cy Young Awards for his mantel.

INDEX

267

G

Gaborik, Marian, 169, 172–173, 262
Gaetti, Gary, 92
Gagliardi, John, 216–219, 220, 220, 223, 224
Gainey, Bob, 83
Gangelhoff, Jan, 202, 204–205
Gant, Ron, 85, 96, 126, 127
Garces, Rich, 142
Gardenhire, Ron, 37, 113
Garnett, Kevin, 77
  Basketball Hall of Fame and, 263–264
  drafting of, 157
  Griffin, Eddie, 246
  Iverson, Allen, 84
  NBA championships and, 152–155
General Mills, 258
Genter, Frances, 193
Gibson-Nagurski Football Complex, 77
Gilliam, John, 56
Gladden, Dan, 93, 97, 133, 135, 145
Goals, best, 169–171
Goaltender, on hockey dream team, 179–180
Gold Gloves, 127–129
Goldsworthy, Bill, 171–172, 260
Goldy Gopher (mascot), 237
Goldy Shuffle, 172

Golf, 190–192, 242, 243
Gonzaga University, 202
Gordon, John, 145
Grant, Bud, 3
  1975 season, 11
  athletic accomplishments, 229–230
  Brown, Bill, 20
  Burns, Jerry, 33–34
  coaching legacy and reputation, 215, 223–224
  Grant, Mike, 218, 219–220
  Krause, Paul, 65
  Lynn, Mike, 26
  Metropolitan Stadium, 21–22
  Purple People Eaters, 50
  retirement of, 37
  stadium names and, 207–208
  Steckel, Les, 17, 18
Grant, Mike, 218–220
Grant, Mudcat, 134, 143–144
Green, Denny, 35–36
  Barnard, Tom, 90
  coaching legacy, 27–29
  Lynn, Mike, 26–27
  NFC Championship Game (1998), 8
  No Room for Crybabies, 35–36
  quotes, 42–44
  Underwood, Dimitrius, 30
Green, Norm, 83, 162–163
Green Bay Packers, 5

ACKNOWLEDGMENTS

This will be a little bit like an acceptance speech at the Oscars, except I won't be thanking the Academy. I would, however, like to thank . . .

Dave Hamilton, the station manager at KQRS, who let me spew opinions and develop an argumentative style over a period of nearly 20 years on the KQRS Morning Show.

Mike Bass, the sports editor at the *St. Paul Pioneer Press*, who allowed me to hone my argumentative skills in print.

Mary Sansevere, who, besides keeping our four kids from pestering me too much when I worked on the book, offered several great ideas for arguments.

Justin Severson, who works at KQRS and also suggested a few arguments.

Rick Alonzo, my co-worker at the *Pioneer Press*, who suggested to Sourcebooks that I would be a suitable author for this book.

Christi Cardenas, who works for the Lazear Agency and made it easy for me to concentrate on writing the 100 arguments.

Shana Drehs, who did a terrific job editing this book.

And . . .

All the athletes, coaches, and team executives whose careers made this book possible.

ABOUT THE AUTHOR

Bob Sansevere has been a sports columnist with the St. Paul *Pioneer Press* for nearly two decades and is a long-time member of the KQRS Morning Show. He began covering Minnesota sports in 1984. Born to loud, opinionated parents, he is genetically predisposed to starting an argument.